The science of social medicine

Alwyn Smith, PH.D, MB, CH.B(Birmingham), DPH(London),
MRCP(Glasgow)
Professor of Social and Preventive Medicine,
University of Manchester

Staples   London

© Alwyn Smith 1968
First published in 1968 by Staples Press
3 Upper James Street Golden Square London W 1
Printed in Great Britain by
The Garden City Press Limited
Letchworth Hertfordshire
SBN: 286 63142 3

The science of social medicine

Contents

Preface   7

Part I   Principles and methods

1   The growth of ideas about community health   11
2   Collection of continuous data on community health   24
3   Methods of analysis   40
4   Special surveys   61

Part II   Areas of current enquiry

5   Present and future problems in community health   79
6   Heredity and community health   94
7   The environment before birth   112
8   Human behaviour as a cause of disease   133
9   The external environment and health   149
10   Disorders of behaviour   166
11   Health and medical care   186
12   Social medicine and medical science   208

References   215
Index   219

Preface

Social medicine, like most other sciences, is characterised as much by its distinctive investigative methods as by its area of concern. This is partly because a particular domain of enquiry may demand a particular kind of technique but also because investigators who have acquired a particular range of skills often continue to seek areas of enquiry which will permit them to exploit them.

The present work, therefore, seeks to convey something of the characteristic research methods of social medicine as well as to indicate the range of subject matter with which this science is concerned. The main structure of the book reflects the range of subject matter, while the treatment, which makes extensive use of examples of actual research, is intended to convey the character of the methods employed.

The first part of the book presents an account of the history of the study of community health and outlines the principal current sources of data and methods of enquiry. The second part deals with the main areas of concern of current research and illustrates these by examples. In general, references to published research are given only when the work is being used as an example.

No attempt has been made to be exhaustive; this would be impossible within the scope of a work of necessarily modest length. In the belief that it is of more interest to convey the characteristic flavour of social medicine enquiry than to present a representative or exhaustive inventory of its academic contributions, the author has simply set down a personal statement of what current research in social medicine seems chiefly to be about. His qualifications to attempt such a statement are simply those of a practising scientist in this field, currently engaged both in teaching and research in social medicine and familiar in a general way with the work of his closer and more remote colleagues.

In Britain, at least, and to some extent internationally,

workers in social medicine are mostly known to one another and are a communicative fraternity who freely exchange information about their current concerns, who argue about how the subject should be presented to students and who write quite voluminously in the appropriate periodicals. The ideas of social medicine are therefore seldom limited to a narrow circle associated with their originators, but rapidly become common currency. It is thus likely that many of the views expressed in this work have not been duly attributed to their authors. The present author is very heavily indebted to his several teachers, to many of his students and to most of his colleagues for any ideas he may have. It is hoped that this acknowledgment of his sources will suffice; any more specific attribution would involve an impossible task of disentanglement.

Part I   Principles and methods

Chapter 1   The growth of ideas about community health

Although the term 'social medicine' has gained a wide currency during the past twenty years, the precise scope of the
subject is not yet widely understood. The term has been used
in two quite distinct senses. In one sense, it is used to describe
a philosophy devoted to the preservation of the liberal traditions in medicine in the face of an inevitably increasing technical sophistication of clinical methods. In its more precise
sense, the term is used to denote the branch of medical science
that is concerned with the study of health and sickness as they
occur in human society and with the factors that determine
their distribution and effect. It is in this latter sense that the
term is used in the present work.

Since the importance of diseases in a society depends on
their duration and on the degree of disability to which they
may give rise, as well as on their frequency and their lethal
effect, it is important in many studies of the disease load borne
by a community, to consider not only the causes of diseases
but also the influences which determine their severity, their
course and their outcome. In recent times, some of the more
important factors determining the outcome of disease have
been the steps that we take to treat or modify it. Social
medicine therefore concerns itself not only with the population
distribution of the causes of diseases and of health but also
with how medical care is organized within society and with
what factors influence its distribution, utilization and effectiveness. In addition, these essentially practical, central preoccupations have widened in their scope, so that social medicine
now embraces a whole range of concerns related to the study
of man as a species and the way in which his biological and
social characteristics affect, or may be adapted to affect, his
survival.

It is for these reasons that the term 'social medicine' is now
generally preferred to the alternative and older term 'epidemiology'. This term too, may be defined as the study of factors

determining the occurrence of diseases in populations. Although the central preoccupation of social medicine is also with problems of the population distribution of diseases, and although therefore, the two items might legitimately be said to deal with a more or less identical domain, the older term retains, for many people, too restricted a connotation, although its use in much the same sense as the newer term of social medicine seems likely to continue for some time.

Whichever term we use, this discipline involves the study of health and disease at the community level and is thus distinct from clinical medicine which is concerned with problems of disease in individuals. It is, of course, easy to press this distinction too far. Social medicine inevitably takes account of the fact that societies are composed of individuals, just as clinical medicine inevitably recognizes that individuals belong to societies. But the distinction is nevertheless important. For an individual, the importance of a disease is fairly simply evaluated; either he or someone near him suffers from the disease or he does not. For societies, on the other hand, most diseases are always present in greater or smaller numbers; their importance is measured by their frequency as well as by their severity. In social medicine, therefore, it is important to be able to distinguish variations in the frequency of diseases, whether these are associated with time, or with season, or with identifiable environments, or with characteristics of the communities between which disease frequency varies. Social medicine cannot therefore exist as a study until a society has achieved a sufficient level of development to permit the recording and counting of disease occurrence, and the detection of variation in its frequency. In a simple society, this capability is generally relatively poorly developed, so that undue disease occurrence is detected only if the occurrence is explosive and of relatively circumscribed duration. These attributes are generally characteristic of outbreaks of certain acute infections, which are therefore often referred to as epidemic diseases. It is not surprising that early epidemiology was largely concerned with these acute infectious diseases and that they were among the first to be singled out for special attention and for special attempts at explanation of their occurrence.

Study of the occurrence of disease in human societies is almost certainly as old as the development of the necessary skills required for the detection of episodes of undue disease prevalence. The urge to explain observed phenomena is probably an inherent human attribute and we know that the most primitive societies evolve elaborate explanations of their recognizable common experience. In very simple societies, explanations of the occurrence of misfortune generally involve the notion of a hostile agency which is frequently represented as a malevolent spirit that inflicts misfortune on mankind out of a largely capricious malice. A system of preventive medicine based on such a view of the causation of outbreaks of disease tends to consist principally of ritual placation of the hostile spirits and is not always notable for its effectiveness.

In slightly more advanced societies the occurrence of misfortune may be seen quite differently. In these societies, diseases, in common with other mass afflictions, are seen as being sent by good spirits rather than by evil ones. Thus, they are interpreted as evidence of divine anger at the unrighteousness of the societies that are afflicted. A system of preventive medicine based on such a view seeks to identify forms of behaviour that are the subject of such divine disapproval, so as to prohibit them. Since the detectable disease outbreaks in relatively primitive societies are mostly of acute infections, whose causes usually directly precede the development of the sickness, they are relatively easily seen to be associated with the forms of behaviour that precipitate them. Such forms of behaviour may be readily categorized as sinful and consequently be prohibited. For example, the eating or drinking of contaminated foods is often simply identifiable as the cause of gastro-intestinal infections, and foods that are commonly involved may be prohibited as unclean. Many primitive systems of hygiene embodied views of this kind and labelled certain habits known to be pathogenic, as sinful. Prohibitions designed to avoid unclean things had the force of orders to avoid sin. Severe illness was regarded as due to extreme sinfulness and merited the exclusion of the afflicted person from society. That such isolation limited the spread of certain diseases would be regarded as confirmation of the view that sin and sinners should be eradicated from society. In particular, early societies generally identified leprosy as a disease meriting immediate exclusion of the sufferer from society. Such a policy was based more on the unpleasantness of the affliction than on any real evidence of high infectivity but similar considerations still influence the public attitude to leprosy in many parts of the world.

We may still recognize a similar type of attitude to disease causation in our own society. However, we now usually exhibit our guilt at communal rather than at personal level. The modern plagues—peptic ulcer, coronary artery disease, lung cancer—are often attributed to a real or imagined sin which our society commits against nature. 'The stress and strain of modern life' is an expression deriving from a similar kind of guilt sense to that which prompted earlier societies to identify misfortune as a punishment for sin.

Greenwood,[1] an epidemiologist of the early twentieth century, published an excellent historical account of the subject and the outline which now follows owes much to his writings.

The first recorded accounts of objective investigation of the population occurrence of disease were published by Hippocrates (c. 460 B.C.). In his 'Epidemics' and in a notebook entitled 'Airs Waters and Places' he provided examples of the use of epidemiological methods which resemble many of the techniques still current today. His system of careful observation of the nature of diseases, together with observations of the places and times in which they occurred, led him to the view that epidemics were to be regarded as more than aggregations of individual disease occurrences. Hippocrates developed the concept of disease entities, varying to some extent between one patient and another, but demonstrating sufficient common characteristics to justify application of a common name and to render profitable the study of diseases as opposed to the more primitive study of sick persons.

Another of the ancient physicians who contributed notably

to our understanding of epidemics was Galen (A.D. 130–210). His concepts of population disease occurrence have lasted well and are surprisingly acceptable at the present day. Galen believed that the generation of community sickness depended on three factors. There was an atmospheric factor; there was a factor related to the susceptibilities of the population's members; and there were also predisposing factors related to the way of life. Thus, Galen had formulated a notion resembling our own concept of immunity, as well as the notion of the importance of socially determined behaviour in the genesis of disease.

After Galen, there was little development over the next fifteen hundred years, although at some stage the notion of disease communicability must have arisen. It is hard to identify the origins of this idea and it was not very clearly formulated until very much later. By the seventeenth century, medicine had become a fairly well organized body of knowledge and the foundations of anatomy and physiology had been well laid. In some countries, medicine had become academically respectable and in a few countries it was also socially respectable. A number of doctors had emerged who might be described as scientists and some aspects of medicine were being subjected to critical scrutiny. However, ideas about the occurrence of disease in society were still restricted by the absence of rigorously systematized information, and no great advances had occurred since Galen's time.

Sydenham (1624–1689) was the next figure of importance in the development of epidemiology. As an epidemiologist, his main contribution was that he resurrected the ideas of Hippocrates in framing the concept of diseases as entities. He believed that not only were diseases recognizable as distinct entities occurring in numbers of the population within circumscribed periods and places, but also that they varied from generation to generation in their importance. He believed that the great plagues of his own time would ultimately pass away and be replaced by new ones of which he had not heard.

Contemporary with Sydenham was a London draper by the name of John Graunt. As a pastime; Graunt collected information from the London Bills of Mortality which periodically itemized the causes of deaths. Graunt tabulated the data, subjected them to simple numerical analysis, scrutinized their plausibility and cautiously interpreted them as evidence of the changing state of community health. His work marked the beginning of a new era. He had hit upon the means whereby quantitative data bearing on community health might be made systematically available and be subjected to analysis. His methods founded a whole new science. For centuries, epidemiology had lacked what the other medical sciences had found much easier to develop, a means of obtaining data that could be used to construct and to test hypotheses.

Graunt's work was widely emulated. In many countries, and particularly in England, the central government recognized the need to systematize such data collection. During the nineteenth century, systematic collection of information on the causes of mortality was intensively developed. In Britain, the General Register Office in England and its counterpart in Scotland, developed their procedures for collecting and publishing tabulated data and commenting on the causes of deaths and their variation with season, time and place. These Annual Reports of the Registrars General constitute a substantial body of data on the occurrence of lethal diseases which still may be made to yield valuable insight into the trends and patterns of public health.

Despite the work of Graunt, and the consequent developments, theoretical epidemiology advanced little until the middle of the nineteenth century. The concepts of the processes of disease occurrence first formulated by Hippocrates had been advanced a little. The concept of infectivity was well established by the end of the eighteenth century but its place in the genesis of epidemics was not clearly understood. We had the beginnings of statistical methods in the collection of data and also in the analytical methods which had been developed in other sciences.

But the most obvious development which revolutionized epidemiology in the nineteenth century was the discovery that micro-organisms were associated with many of the major killing diseases of the time. This discovery soon dominated the whole field of epidemiology and there was an almost total neglect of other potent factors in the genesis of disease. The triumphs of the micro-biologists in the latter half of the century seemed a never-ending succession and the impression grew that sooner or later all disease would prove to be due to living micro-organisms.

However, there were several other lines of research development proceeding in a less spectacular way. These had less impact during the nineteenth century than they have had in the twentieth century as we have turned from the field of communicable disease to that of the non-communicable disease plagues of our own day.

The recognition that diseases were far from randomly dispersed throughout communities seems in retrospect to have been a most important feature of nineteenth-century epidemiology. The association of poverty with disease and death, and the association of poverty and disease with 'filth' were well recognized by many early workers. Not all these observations were readily attributable to simple associations between bacteria and ways of living. The attempt at systematic examination of disease occurrences began to bear fruit long before bacteriologists had isolated the organisms involved. John Snow and William Budd had worked out most of the important facts about the genesis of cholera epidemics before it had been established that they had a microbial cause. The story of the cholera epidemic in Broad Street, London, is often quoted. Snow's observations of the affected patients and of their place of residence and source of water, led to his incrimination of the Broad Street pump as the source of the infection.

Budd had similarly explained the mode of transmission of typhoid fever and was later to clinch the argument for the role of water in the transmission of both diseases long before their causal organisms had been identified.

But perhaps the most permanently important development at this time was the work of Farr and Ross and others who developed from the pioneer work of Graunt a system of statistical epidemiology. Farr was the first medical statistician to the

General Register Office in England. In his second annual report appeared the following:

'Epidemics appear to be generated at intervals in unhealthy places, spread, go through a regular course, and decline; but of the cause of their evolutions no more is known than of the periodical paroxysms of ague. The body in its diseases as well as its functions, observes a principle of periodicity; its elements pass through prescribed cycles of changes, and the diseases of nations are subject to similar variations. If the latent cause of epidemics cannot be discovered, the mode in which it operates may be investigated. The laws of its action may be determined by observation, as well as the circumstances in which epidemics arise or by which they may be controlled.'

Farr followed this by an examination of the quarterly totals of deaths from smallpox showing that these approximated to a regular mathematical series. Throughout his life he sought to show that the distribution of disease was describable in mathematical terms and that the descriptions might afford a clue to the processes responsible for the mathematical forms observed.

Farr's work bore fruit. Towards the end of the nineteenth century and during the twentieth, epidemiologists such as Brownlee, Pearson, Ross, Greenwood and Frost refined and adapted quantitative methods in epidemiology. Much of the pioneer work was done against a background which could scarcely have been less encouraging. The success of the bacteriologists in identifying and describing bacteria came to be regarded as the central achievement in public health. Greenwood, describing epidemiology at the turn of the century, wrote: 'It came to be believed, is still believed by a majority, that epidemiology from the scientific point of view is a mere appendix of bacteriology, that when the means of infection and the vehicles of infection have been identified the problem of an outbreak of herd sickness is solved.'

Several developments brought epidemiology back to its traditional concern with the occurrence of disease in society and with the characteristics of affected groups. The realization that the study of bacteria was failing to explain the whole problem of community disease had first been expressed by Koch, the discoverer of the tubercle bacillus. The great influenza epidemic of 1919 spread this realization further. Classical bacteriological epidemiology could offer no adequate explanation of this disaster.

And so the simple view, that disease was a relatively uncomplicated result of the invasion of the human body by micro-organisms, came to be abandoned. The newer concept was an ecological one in which man and microbe were seen as living together in a state of balanced symbiosis, largely controlled by the characteristics of their common environment. Disease was seen as a disturbance in this equilibrium which adversely affected both host and parasitic disease agent. Disease outbreaks were seen as the result of a change either in the immunity of the population, or in the virulence of the organism, or in the environment that maintained their symbiosis. Changes in human immunity may occur either because of changes in the intensity of exposure to infecting agents or because of migrations which may introduce new population members with different levels of immunity to particular disease organisms. For example, the immigration of rural people to an urban environment in search of work, may expose them to infections against which they have little immunity, but whose agents are commonly parasitic among the urban dweller whose immunity is high. Tuberculosis in the cities of developing countries provides an example of such a mechanism in operation, and in the early years of the present century a similar situation is said to have occurred among the policemen of Glasgow who were often recruited from Highland areas where exposure to tuberculosis was minimal. There is less evidence that the virulence of organisms may be subject to changes which might precipitate disease outbreaks. The only well authenticated example in relation to a common disease is that of scarlet fever, whose seriousness has periodically changed in consequence of changes in the causal organism. However, the ecological view of disease occurrence was able more satisfactorily to explain a number of features of the behaviour of communicable diseases than had the simple views that preceded it. Thus, by the first quarter of the twentieth century, attempts to explain the community distribution of diseases had led to the development of an epidemiology based on ecological concepts and equipped with effective numerical investigational techniques.

But, in more recent years, these concepts have again been found inadequate. The importance of the infective diseases has declined. The great social and economic advances of the nineteenth and early twentieth centuries transformed the environment and swept away the menace of the enteric fevers and of cholera and smallpox. As the importance of these former plagues declined, so the remaining, non-infective diseases assumed greater prominence. As we shall see later, it is also clear that these newer diseases have increased in absolute frequency. The change in the age composition of the population, brought about by the reduction in early mortality, brought an increase in the degenerative and other diseases of later life. New hazards were introduced to the environment. Industry has brought toxic and accident risks. The greater use of machinery has increased the total of deaths from injury. Although there have been attempts to accommodate our explanations of the genesis of the new diseases within the older conceptual framework which attributed disease occurrence to the effects of interaction between host, agent and their common environment, these attempts are mostly clumsy and unhelpful and are generally being abandoned. New ideas are now required if we are to continue to advance our understanding of disease causation.

While these changes in the causes and kinds of sickness have been taking place, medicine itself has changed. After centuries of restriction to the roles of diagnostician and comforter, the physician has recently become equipped with effective weapons of prevention and treatment. The old conception of medicine as a priestly relationship between doctor and patient has died. It has been replaced by a conception of medicine as a social service which is capable of being effective, and whose effectiveness will depend on its organization and on its suitability to the clearly defined needs of the population. Thus, man's attempts to understand the occurrence of sickness in his own society have acquired a new urgency in the context of present needs.

Today, social medicine is well established as an academic discipline in the medical schools of the world. It has developed as the science that is concerned with community health. Its present concerns differ sharply from those which engaged the attention of its predecessors because the diseases to which we are subject have changed, because our understanding of human society has increased, and because powerful new investigational methods are now available.

Social medicine today, is concerned with the provision of an account of the health of the population, and with the origins of the current situation and with how it may be expected to develop. Although it is principally concerned, like all sciences, to become progessively more quantitative in its techniques and conclusions, it cannot escape the necessity to employ non-numerical techniques in the investigation of problems to which such methods are more appropriate. Social medicine has recruited a range of workers having their earlier experience and training in a wide variety of population as well as medical sciences, and we are extremely fortunate in the rich armoury of skills, ideas and methods which this science has thereby come to command. These skills and techniques have frequently to be adapted to the special needs of social medical enquiry. Few workers would claim a comprehensive understanding of all its problems or of the techniques which may be brought to bear upon them. It is usual, indeed, for investigators to specialize within the field and to restrict their activities to a particular range of problems and related investigational techniques. In particular, those who prefer to study the causation of diseases, often do not engage in research into the community provision of medical care or into the area which might be described as medical sociology. But academic departments of social medicine contain individuals working in all these fields as well as in the application of population methods to the study of human biology. There is a substantial, and perhaps growing body of investigators, who believe that these distinctions are merely matters of current personal preference and that workers in social medicine may profitably turn their attention to any of the questions which relate to sickness and health in human society. Indeed, there is much to be said for ceasing to draw distinctions which often have the effect of restricting the conceptual scope of the investigator as well as of his research. For example, to state that cigarette smoking is a major cause of lung cancer, although quite true so far as it goes, does not help us to control this disease unless we are also aware of the complex influences that determine indulgence in the smoking habit and which have effectively frustrated attempts to dissuade people from smoking. Studies directed towards quantifying the phenomenon of resistance to anti-smoking campaigns are therefore studies in the causation of cancer.

The influences which determine a society's experience of disease are naturally complex. It is usually easier to study the pathogenic effects of the physical environment inhabited by a society, than to examine the importance of inter-personal relationships in determining the effective quality of the medical care that is available. This may well mean that it is more profitable to tackle the former kind of problem first, since it is usually better to tackle simple problems before proceeding to difficult ones. But it does not mean that the former kinds of influence play a greater part in determining the health of communities or that we should neglect major factors in public health simply because their investigation is difficult. Unless we can appraise the whole range of determinants of population health we are in a poor position to decide what is most important to investigate.

The burden of disease borne by a society can no longer be thought of as being determined simply by factors which cause diseases to arise in individuals, or by the influences which in turn determine the distribution of such pathogenic factors in human society. The prevalence of disease and disability is also determined by factors that influence the outcome of diseases or the duration of their course. These include medical and social intervention directed towards curtailing disease duration or towards modifying disability, and the factors that affect the availability of such intervention and its utilization. Poliomyelitis is a more serious disease problem in some societies than in others not only because it arises more frequently, but also because it is less well treated and the disabilities to which it gives rise result in a greater degree of social and personal dysfunction. The diseases of ageing are more important in some societies than in others, not simply because they occur with greater frequency but because the isolated condition of the elderly leads to their causing greater disability and to their coming less readily to medical attention. It is possible, in Britain, for people to die of minor foot maladies because the old people who incur them are isolated from those who might bring them to medical attention and who might prevent the progressive immobilisation which leads eventually to the patients becoming bedfast and to their dying from hypostatic pneumonia. In a population in which a substantial proportion of people are old and living alone, this is as important a social medical problem as many more spectacularly interesting diseases with simple physical or infective causes.

Social medicine is the science which seeks to examine and interpret the phenomena of sickness and health as they occur in human society and to examine the determinants of the patterns of disease that are encountered. Its range is wide, but it is not, in this respect, unique. A similar need to integrate a wide range of skills in the investigation of complex problems occurs, for example, in molecular biology. There is undoubtedly room for at least the range of interests currently displayed by its academic departments, even although it may well be desirable for each of them to pause occasionally to enquire where it is going.

Chapter 2   Collection of continuous data on community health

Over the past one hundred and fifty years most of the nations
of the world have developed systematic procedures for collecting information on the state of community health. These
routine procedures are augmented, to a varying extent in
different countries, by special studies which may be undertaken by public agencies or by academic research bodies in
medical schools or other institutions. The national procedures
are important principally for the scale on which they may be
mounted but also because they are usually conducted continuously. In most countries, these procedures include some
systematic collection of data on the causes of death, and in
many countries there are at least simple statistics of hospital
admissions and of cases of the principal infectious diseases,
as well as some data on one or more of the individual diseases
that are of special importance in that society. All help to
provide a picture of the state of health in the community and
are generally justified in terms of an acknowledged, but often
unexamined, need for such information. In the present context,
it may be useful to consider the actual and potential value of
such health statistics as basic data for social medical enquiry
before proceeding to an account of what is usually collected
and how its collection is being developed.

Uses of continuous data
National statistics on health may be used in the investigation of
problems of planning of health and medical services, in
studies of the aetiology and natural history of diseases and in
studies of the effects of medical and social intervention on the
state of community health.

1. Planning of services. There are no parts of the world
where available resources are adequate to meet all imaginable
demands for health and medical care and there are many
places where resources fall very far short of what would be

required to meet even the more clamant needs. This will doubtless always be so, since it will always be possible to imagine a better world than the one we inhabit, and while we can envisage it we shall inevitably desire it. This means that it is important to use available resources as well as we are able and to do so in the light of the most careful appraisal of current and predictable needs and of how they may most effectively be met. This proposition may seem self-evident. It certainly would have done, a hundred years ago, to the early workers in public health whose optimistic rationalism inspired the beginnings of modern preventive medicine. But the problem is less simple than it appears. In the early years of preventive medicine, public health programmes were chiefly directed against a small range of easily definable disease problems and the data needed for planning were relatively easy to obtain. The great expansion of the scope of public health work that has taken place in the past one hundred years has increased tremendously the range and complexity of the data required; but the facilities for collecting and analysing them at national level have shown no commensurate expansion. Because of this, those responsible for planning health services have often been forced to do without an adequate numerical basis for their work and have generally learned, therefore, to depend more on intuitive processes than on rigorously numerical appraisal of needs and effects. Since they have been reasonably successful in this they have now naturally come to ignore the need for a better basis for their decisions and frequently reject what help can be provided.

Planning must be based on prediction, and although it is important to bear in mind that prediction is always beset with the possibility of error, it is also important to recognize the possibility of assessing priorities with at least some objectivity and sometimes of making a surprisingly useful appraisal of trends from examination of relatively simple data. It is possible, for example, to come to some sort of useful decision concerning the likely relative importance of preventive and curative medicine in the forthcoming decades and to base plans for the recruitment and training of doctors and other medical workers accordingly.[2]

In the shorter term, a more detailed type of information is often needed for planning. For example, in many western countries in recent years, there has been a change in reproductive behaviour with a tendency to younger marriage and parenthood. This raises the birth rate in the immediate period in which it happens, but we do not yet know whether the total number of births will be raised in the long term by the increased opportunity for child-bearing which an early start confers. The question is important to those who have charge of planning for maternity hospital building and recruitment, to the midwifery profession and to others concerned with providing for maternal and child care.

Another example concerns prediction of the likely effect of medical advances on the need for hospital accommodation. For example, innovations in the use of drugs in treating mental illness have been associated with a reduction in the average duration of hospital stay. We need to discover whether this will reduce the need for mental hospital beds or raise it. At present we do not know whether the new drugs will reduce total demand for hospital admission, by shortening the average duration of mental illness, or will increase it by popularizing the hospital treatment of illnesses that are now usually left untreated for lack of any useful remedy.

In a different area, there is a need for detailed demographic information on the availability of potential recruits to the medical and nursing professions. Much of the present shortage of nurses in Britain, for example, might have been foreseen, and other plans might have been made, had appropriate studies been carried out sufficiently early.

Planning is an unpopular activity, of course, since it implies some curtailment of general freedom. In particular, the medical profession is averse to direction since it usually does not see the need and fears loss of the privileges which are safeguarded by retention of a free bargaining position. Certainly, the fact that the sickness needs of patients are met at all in most societies, is attributable to the unplanned response of the medical profession to the sickness it encounters. But it is also evident that this is not an effective basis for planning of services. For example, the common disabling diseases usually receive far less attention than do the spectacular rarities. There are long waiting lists in Britain for the surgical repair of herniae and of uterine prolapse, but there is no great difficulty in getting into hospital for investigation of the rare diseases that interest many doctors.

2. The causes and natural history of diseases. It is less often realized that nationally collected data may be used for purposes of research into the causes and natural history of diseases, but there are two good reasons why such data provide an important source of research information. The first is that national governments are uniquely in a position to collect data on the extensive scale that is required for the solution of many of the problems of the present day. The second is that since aetiological research is mainly directed towards the identification of suitable techniques for disease prevention and that since the organization of preventive techniques is almost always necessarily performed at government level, it seems efficient for collection of the appropriate data and their analysis, to be performed by the same authorities that will need to act on the results.

Clearly, the complete exploitation of available data cannot be wholly achieved by national health statistical agencies and national data should be, and usually are, made available to other research workers.

Detailed examples of the use of such data for aetiological research will be discussed extensively, later in the present work; but it may be useful to consider some of them briefly at this point. The most important areas in which they lie are: investigation of the effects of the changing physical environment in which we all live; study of the influence of changing human behaviour; and development of more effective methods for early diagnosis of disease.

The main adverse elements in our present physical environment are those associated with industry and its processes, those arising from transport, and those arising from medical treatment and diagnostic procedures. In nearly all cases, an important element in their study is the accumulation of data over long periods of exposure and for long periods afterwards. Examples include the association between bladder cancer and work in the aniline dye industry, and the influence of prenatal X-ray exposure on the later development of malignant disease in childhood (see chapter 7).

Research into the causes of diseases having their origin wholly or partly in personal behaviour is important today (see chapter 8) and involves the need to examine disease occurrence against the background of a knowledge of cultural, political, economic and other social factors that determine behaviour. Since specific manipulation of human behaviour is generally inefficient and may always be held to be undesirable, direct prevention of these diseases may always be difficult if not impossible. It is generally expected that progress in the prevention of the effect of these diseases will be by means of improved treatment which may depend for its effectiveness on earlier diagnosis, possibly before the onset of symptoms. The development of methods of early detection and their eventual application may need the large scale enquiry that only national health statistical data can provide.

It is still necessary for government agencies to operate procedures for the early detection of outbreaks of disease. Although in many countries, the characteristically epidemic communicable diseases are less important than formerly, they remain important problems in the world in general and may still occur occasionally even in the countries where they are generally rare. Indeed, their lesser frequency makes it more important to keep adequate detection systems in operation since general immunity, whether natural or artificial, may well be low. For example, when smallpox occurred more commonly in Britain than it does today, a much larger proportion of the population was adequately protected by vaccination. An outbreak occurring now involves the need for large scale vaccination programmes in the affected areas and the efficient organization of this depends on an adequate intelligence service being available. But hazards other than the communicable diseases may occur in epidemic form. Two striking examples in recent years have been retrolental fibroplasia, an eye disease leading to blindness, which occurred among premature babies who had received liberal oxygen therapy shortly after birth, and the outbreak of limb defects among babies whose mothers had received thalidomide during pregnancy. In the first example, the cause took several years to identify; in the latter case it took considerably less. But we still require to maintain and improve our technique for the detection of undue occurrences of disease in the population and the organizational and analytical problems remain formidable.

3. Evaluation of the effect of services. Governmental acceptance of an increasing responsibility for the provision of health and medical services has been a feature of most countries' development during the present century. This responsibility carries the concomitant one of subjecting to continuous scrutiny the functioning of these services. Continuous scrutiny is, of course, inherent in good management but there is a need for additional periodic evaluation of special health and medical programmes. Such studies are usually built in as part of the programmes they are designed to evaluate and the collection of suitable data will usually flow from the organization of the programme itself. Evaluation may be simple or complex. For example, at its simplest, it might involve no more than periodic examination of the numbers of cases of tuberculosis that are notified during a programme for the eradication of that disease. Similar problems exist in relation to evaluation of the effect of routine tests for early cancer of the uterine cervix, although the problem is less easy since the expected effects will be less marked. More complex problems arise when the need occurs to measure the use of available services and to identify the factors which may influence such use. Studies of this kind are relatively new and call for the development of methods for evaluating the quality of medical care being received and of methods for the quantitative study of the socially determined attitudes which may influence public acceptance of services. Studies of this kind are of relatively recent development in most countries and the extent to which they are sponsored or carried out by governmental agencies is very variable throughout the world.

Types of national and regional data
As we have seen, the earliest generally available data on disease in the community derived from certified opinions on the causes of death. Even today, mortality statistics form a very important source of data for government agencies and for research workers. At an earlier period, these statistics were of even greater value because so many of the socially important diseases were commonly fatal and the deaths occurred, in many cases, after illnesses of quite short duration. Thus, the information derived from statistics of causes of death, gave a reasonably up-to-date account of the occurrence of serious disease.

Most countries of the world impose certain formalities to be observed in relation to death. It is usually incumbent on a close relative of the dead person to register the fact of death with the appropriate authority. In many countries, permission to dispose of the body by burial or cremation is made dependent on registration, and it seems that in most countries, registration of death is carried out promptly after its occurrence. Most countries also require the registration of a properly authenticated opinion as to the cause of death. In countries where there are few doctors, this certification of cause may be carried out by police, by magistrates or headmen or by other non-medical officials. In such countries the cause is necessarily given in simple terms which may distinguish only between natural causes, dangerous infectious disease and violence. In countries where it is usual for fatal illnesses to have been attended by doctors, it is usual to require a medical opinion as to the cause of death. There are differences in the procedures to be followed when the doctor is unable or unwilling to give an opinion, but in most cases, in most countries, medical opinions as to the cause of death are given in the form of the International Death Certificate. This certificate was adopted by the World Health Organization and its use enjoined on member countries, so as to permit a reasonable degree of comparability between the mortality statistics of different countries.

It would, of course, be possible to give an opinion on the cause of a death in a variety of different ways. For example, in the case of a man run over by a 'bus and who died of crush injuries of the chest, the cause of death might be given as asphyxia, loss of blood, cessation of heart beat, impatience in crossing the road, faulty brakes on the 'bus, personality defects of either man or 'bus driver, the pressure of an urgent appointment, the invention of petrol engines, and so on. The International Certificate has, as its basic principle, an attempt to identify not only the manner of dying but also its underlying cause in terms of diseases or injuries which might be considered to be of public health importance.

The present International Certificate attempts to distinguish between the fatal sequence of events and the existence of contributory or associated conditions. The following example illustrates the use of the certificate.

CAUSE OF DEATH (Please print clearly)	
I	**I**
Disease or condition directly leading to death* (a)	Peritonitis
due to (or as a consequence of)	
Antecedent causes (b)	Perforation of duodenal ulcer
Morbid conditions, if any, giving rise to the above cause, the underlying condition to be stated last	
due to (or as a consequence of)	
(c)	Peptic ulcer of the duodenum
II	**II**
Other significant conditions *contributing to the death, but not related to the disease or condition causing it.*	Chronic Bronchitis with emphysema

This certificate relates to a person who died of a perforated duodenal ulcer with peritonitis and whose death may have been influenced by his also having chronic bronchitis with emphysema. The underlying cause is considered to be peptic ulcer of the duodenum and it is to this cause that the death would be assigned for purposes of national mortality statistics.

Experience with this certificate in many countries of the world indicates that its use is convenient and meaningful in the case of deaths occurring at all ages except the very young and the very old. In the case of deaths in the first few hours or days of life, the cause is often multiple and indeterminate and the use of the certificate is very difficult. The same may apply to deaths among the very old, in whom several disease processes may be present and death may occur peacefully during sleep with no clear indication of its cause. Post-mortem examination would usually be unjustified in such a case and might very well not be helpful in determining the cause.

In many countries, where the bulk of deaths may occur among people who are neither very young nor very old, the difficulty may not be very important, but increasingly in the developed countries, death is becoming relatively uncommon except among the very young or the very old. In these countries, attention is being given to how to deal with the difficulty. One solution would be to abandon the concept of the underlying cause of death and to require only that the disease conditions present at the time of death be recorded on the certificate. Statistical tabulation of mortality data would then show multiple causes and the numbers of deaths in which each condition was present would be shown. Experiments have been carried out with such methods and there are many difficulties. Nevertheless, it seems likely that the present International Certificate may be abandoned in the next twenty years and be replaced by one which simply permits the recording of all disease conditions present at the time of death.

Statistical analysis of the data on causes of death usually consists of tabulation of underlying causes of death by sex, age, area and season together with additional special tabulations of the mortality in different occupations or in other identifiable population groups which may be of current national interest. In Britain, the tables are published in Annual Reports of the Registrars General of England and Wales and of Scotland. These Reports present information in such a way that it may be used by research workers. In addition to the major Annual Reports, weekly and quarterly publications appear, containing preliminary data.

The early establishment of procedures for collecting, analysing and publishing statistics on mortality influenced the development of methods for obtaining and dealing with data on non-fatal illness. The earliest of these procedures for morbidity statistics, as they are usually called, was probably in relation to communicable disease. Because of the need for local and central health authorities to be informed early of the presence of outbreaks of infectious disease, many countries introduced compulsory reporting of cases of specified diseases. Obligation to report was placed on the doctor who treated the disease, and in Britain, reporting was to the local Medical Officer of Health. National lists of notifiable diseases were established, generally on the basis that oubreaks of the included diseases were matters requiring public action. Selection of the list of diseases was not always very rational, however. For example, in England and Wales, measles is a notifiable disease and its notification costs the nation about £100,000 each year. Notification of some diseases is notoriously incomplete. In general, those diseases that are no longer considered by doctors as a major threat to public health are under-notified. Diseases which are still thought to be important (e.g. tuberculosis, poliomyelitis) are probably fairly fully notified. In the case of poliomyelitis, the number of initial notifications usually exceeds the true number of cases, since cases only suspected of being poliomyelitis are often notified. This situation is corrected when final statistics are published, since only confirmed cases are included.

The most important source of statistical data on morbidity in most countries is from hospital statistics. In most countries of the world, information is now nationally collected on the number of admissions to general hospitals and in many countries similar information is available from other kinds of hospitals. Many countries also collect data on out-patient attendances. In most cases the available data are confined to the numbers admitted and sometimes these are tabulated by diagnosis, by type of specialty or by region. Usually, national

data are compiled from tabular returns sent by individual
hospitals, but in several countries more elaborate systems are
in operation. Some of these are worth considering in more
detail.

In Scotland, a return is made for each patient discharged
from a general hospital, and in England and Wales a similar
return is made for every tenth person discharged. These
returns contain details of the person admitted—his age, sex,
marital state and occupation—information on his illness and
on its treatment and information on the duration of stay, the
type of specialty, the source of admission and the disposal on
discharge. In both countries the central health authorities
collect and analyse the data, using the resulting analyses for
administrative information purposes and for publishing annual
tabulations.

For patients admitted to mental hospitals, data are usually
collected on admission as well as at discharge since many
patients remain for a considerable time in mental hospitals
and up-to-date data are needed on trends in admissions.

In the United States, collection of corresponding information is made on a sample basis. The sampling procedure
permits selective collection of data, so that areas of especial
interest may be given special attention, and permits an economical use of clerical and other resources in collecting the
data.

In many countries, special statistical studies are routinely
made of diseases which are especially important. In many
tropical countries, for example, studies are made of malaria,
of hookworm, of trachoma and of other parasitic diseases. In
most countries of the temperate regions special studies are
maintained of cancer. The usual practice is to arrange for
the registration of all cases of cancer seen at hospitals. Cases
are followed at annual or other regular intervals and the data
are collected and analysed, mainly so as to identify the chief
influences that affect survival and the trends in survival that
occur over the years.

More recently, many countries have begun to collect systematic data on the occurrence of congenital malformations. Such

systems were mostly inspired by the recent epidemic of thalidomide-induced limb defects which had very considerable publicity and which aroused health authorities to the possibility of epidemics of diseases other than the traditional infectious ones.

In recent years, two main criticisms have been made of national provisions for collecting and analysing data on community health. The first has been that statistics deriving from hospitals and from death certificates relate only to a limited range of community ill-health; the second criticism has been that such statistics have an episode of sickness as their basis rather than a sick person.

The first criticism has been countered to some extent by the development of statistical reporting of morbidity from sources other than the hospitals and special clinics. First, there have been a number of attempts to collect nation-wide data on consultations with general practitioners. This, of course, poses many problems of organization. In many countries, general practitioners do not welcome the additional tasks that such systems of data-collection may involve. Various procedures have been devised for reducing or avoiding the additional labour. One technique is to employ such records as are already inevitably made; for example, in the writing of prescriptions for drugs and in certifying sickness in connexion with claims under social security insurance schemes. Such sources of data have the disadvantage that they do not relate to all morbidity but to a portion of it treated in a particular way. The morbidity included may therefore be unrepresentative. There is also the problem that diagnoses may be misleadingly recorded on documents that may have to be handed to the patients. Another technique is to use samples of general practitioners and to ask each to report the morbidity encountered over a short period of time. If a large number of doctors are each reporting the morbidity encountered for a single day, a picture may be built up from their reports, of the total morbidity being encountered by doctors. The representativeness of the picture will depend on a suitably organized schedule of reporting and a suitable sampling procedure. Such methods may be valuable for the light they may throw on morbidity being treated by general practitioners.

But not all morbidity is treated. In many countries, an important proportion of total sickness remains untreated, either because there are not enough doctors to treat it or because patients elect not to seek treatment. We have little idea how important this untreated morbidity may be because it remains largely unknown. In several countries, attempts have been made to investigate the matter.

Surveys of total population sickness are frequently conducted in countries where particular diseases present major problems and where cases do not automatically come to medical attention. Surveys of the prevalence of malaria, of worm infestation and of other gross disabilities are a regular feature of the work of health authorities in many tropical countries. In temperate countries the problems are often greater because there may be no single important disease and no simple diagnostic tests. In Britain, several years ago, attempts were made to study the community prevalence of morbidity by regular interviews of a sample of the population concerning its state of health during the preceding two months. These surveys were eventually discontinued. They had provided a great deal of useful information as well as permitting the identification and appraisal of many of the more important difficulties which are encountered in such surveys. Since then, other countries have developed more elaborate methods. In the United States, for example, a permanent interview survey is conducted on a sample of the population. The sample is selected so as to maximize the information available in areas of especial importance and many methodological studies have been carried out on the efficiency of the sampling procedures used, on appropriate methods for analysis of the data and on the validity of the interview methods that are employed. The interview survey has been augmented by an additional survey which is based on medical examination of population samples. These examinations are carried out by comprehensive teams of physicians, biochemists, serologists and others and use is made of mobile caravans which provide the accommodation for the examinations. The caravans cover the country area by area, and the sampling techniques are chosen so as to permit an economical distribution of the work and travelling. At present, the surveys are limited to particular age groups of the population whose health is especially interesting to the health authorities.

A development of the interview method that has been employed in several countries (e.g. Hungary and Japan) relies on the use of a specially prepared recording form which resembles a diary. Sampled households are visited and supplied with these diaries in which they are asked to record their daily state of health for a short ensuing period. Interviewers call during the period to deal with any problems that may have arisen and they call again finally to collect the completed records. Such records are supplemented by more conventional records of hospital and clinic attendances that may have been made. Countries employing such methods are generally satisfied that they furnish useful data that could not be obtained from other sources.

The problem, that most sources of health statistical data focus attention on sickness events rather than on sick persons, has been recognized for a long time. Until relatively recently there was no urgent consideration of how to solve this problem, partly because suitable techniques were lacking and partly because the diseases that were prevalent and important did not seem to justify it. The acute and communicable diseases with which health authorities were chiefly concerned in the past, are generally determined by immediately antecedent causes and have immediately subsequent consequences. It was therefore enough to collect data at the time of the disease occurrence and possible to record simultaneously a simple history of the causal and consequential circumstances. But much of the disease experience we encounter today has causes and consequences at a time remote from that of the disease occurrence. In addition, many of the important diseases are chronic and pursue an episodic course. It has become much more important to take a longer term view of disease and to examine the whole medical history of individual members of society and to collect and analyse statistical data relating to the persons who are sick rather than to their separate episodes of sickness. In addition, the increasing importance (as we shall see later) of genetically determined diseases makes it desirable to examine the familial distribution of disease. This requires that we collate the sickness records of related individuals. Electronic computers will make these kinds of analyses possible, and will greatly facilitate examinations which previously required laborious assembly of related records. Techniques for performing this record linkage and for exploiting the resulting data have been developed in several centres. A most interesting project is that of Acheson[3] in Oxford who is arranging to collate records relating to births, deaths, cancer registrations, hospital admissions and other data on individuals in the Oxford area and to analyse the resulting data on the long term sickness histories of individuals. It has proved possible to collate and analyse the data by computer without the need for other scrutiny of the individual records. In the office of the Registrar General for Scotland, the present author has used similar techniques to study the familial concentration of causes of stillbirth and infant death. There is no doubt that methods of this kind will add a new usefulness to national and regional health statistics but their development poses many problems which have yet to be solved.

There is, in fact, little doubt that techniques for the large scale study of community health are about to be developed immensely. The particular circumstance that has fostered this development has been the introduction of electronic computers. These devices permit the handling, storage and analysis of data on a scale which has previously been unimaginable. They permit a flexibility in data collection and analysis which will transform the tasks of central health statistics agencies by permitting the specific examination of immediately relevant questions rather than the annual compilation of volumes of tables for consultation if and when required. Computers permit the automation of much of the laborious process of data recording and enormously increase the mathematical power of data analysis as well as transforming the speed of the processes involved. Their principal drawback is their expense. This applies not only to the machinery, or 'hardware' as it is usually called, but also to the 'software', which includes the programs of instructions which must be compiled for computers before they can work at all. These programs, representing many man-hours of highly skilled labour, are at least as expensive as the machines themselves. For many countries, a full exploitation of the opportunities which computers can afford would be prohibitively expensive, but it is hoped that eventually this problem will be solved by international co-operation. Countries without their own resources might hire the use of established machines whether on the basis of national negotiation or under the sponsorship of an international body. Such proposals have been put to the World Health Organization and are no doubt receiving attention.

An important new principle in national health statistics is that they should be directly relevant to defined problems. Frequently, at present, they are not very useful because they lack this relevance; but the fact that some countries have useful and lively data demonstrates to others the possibilities that are available. Computers may be expected to end the era when health statistics were dry and uninteresting tables, published annually in a book relating to the year before last, and be expected to bring in a newer concept of health statistics as a live numerical commentary on the state of community health and the effectiveness with which it is being controlled and advanced.

Chapter 3   Methods of analysis

Analysis of data on the population distribution of disease is almost always directed towards the comparison of disease occurrence between identifiable groups of people. Such comparisons are made either for the purpose of posing useful hyptheses or for testing them. The kinds of hypotheses with which social medicine is concerned are very various; the occurrence of disease in society is affected by many different influences. But most hypotheses involve the concept that the amount of disease occurring among a group of people may be related to characteristics of the group or of its particular situation in time or space and that variation between groups in their disease experience may reflect differences between the groups or their environments that may be thought of as determinants of disease. For example, malaria is much more common among the inhabitants of tropical countries than of most other areas of the world. The reason for this is now known to be chiefly related to the influence of the climate upon the kinds and numbers of mosquitoes with which people have to live and upon those habits of both men and insects which influence the mosquitoes' choice of which species to bite. Another quite different example is coronary artery disease, which is much commoner in temperate regions than in tropical. This may be explained by the different kind of life and choice of diet which characterizes the people of different climatic regions. Much less well understood examples include variations between communities in the frequency of congenital malformations, or of multiple sclerosis, or of schizophrenia or of cancers of the various anatomical sites. In many cases, the variations are well documented and the social and environmental associations of the variation are well recognized; in some cases such knowledge has led to clear hypotheses about disease causation, while in other cases the associations remain baffling.

Generally speaking, and for obvious reasons, major variations in disease experience between nationally or continentally distinguishable groups of people are easily recognizable. Their detailed causes are often less easy to investigate. Smaller differences between the disease experience of only slightly dissimilar groups are often very difficult to explain. The shift of viewpoint from the larger to the smaller scale has usually to be accompanied by a more detailed type of examination and the construction and testing of relevant hypotheses is similarly affected.

However, a means is required in both cases of expressing quantitatively the disease experience of human groups. We cannot simply rely on counting the number of cases of disease, since the size of the populations or groups to be compared may differ. For example, the annual number of road accident deaths in England is very much greater than it is in Scotland. This is not to be explained by differences in driving habits or in the states of the roads in the two countries; it is clearly very substantially due to the nearly ten-fold difference in the size of the two populations; in England, there are some ten times as many people at risk of dying in a road accident. This notion of a population at risk is an important one, since it provides the basis of a simple and convenient index of differences in disease experience. We may compare the relative risks in different population groups of becoming ill or of being ill or of dying. These risks may be expressed as the observed proportion of a population that becomes ill or dies during a period of time or the proportion actually sick at a point in time. These proportions are usually called rates and the various different kinds of rates will now be considered.

For many purposes, we need to know the risk of becoming ill in a particular population during a particular period. To calculate the rate that expresses this risk, we need to know the number of new cases in the population during the defined period of time and the number in the population during the period. We can then express the risk in terms of the proportion of the population becoming sick. This proportion is called an incidence or inception rate. It is usual to express the rate in a convenient form such as a percentage, or more commonly, a rate per 1,000 or per 100,000 of the population. For example, if 20 cases of a disease began during a year among a population of 5,000 people we should say that the incidence rate for the year in that population was 4 per 1,000. It is quite common to speak of an annual incidence of 4 per 1,000 and to omit the word 'rate'. The choice of whether to express a rate as a rate per 1,000, or per 100,000 or per million is chiefly guided by the desire to avoid decimal places on the one hand or unhelpful zeros on the other. In the example used above the rate could be expressed as 0·4 per cent or 4,000 per million but the choice of 4 per 1,000 seems more generally convenient.

Incidence rates are commonly used when we wish to consider diseases of short duration, or when attention is being focused on the circumstances surrounding the onset of disease, as is the case generally in studies of causation. But there are many occasions when incidence rates are unhelpful or difficult to employ. For many chronic diseases whose onset is insidious and ill defined, or whose duration is so long that it is the current burden of the disease in a society that is of interest, we need a measure of the risk of *being* ill rather than of *becoming* ill. The proportion of the population suffering from an illness at a defined point of time is the more useful rate in these cases and is called the prevalence rate. As in the case of incidence rates,the word 'rate' is often omitted as being generally understood. Prevalence rates are calculated and expressed in manner similar to that employed in incidence rates; the number of persons sick at a defined time is divided by the number in the population at that time and the result expressed as a per cent or other suitable rate. Prevalence rates are much used in studies of such chronic diseases as anaemia, chronic bronchitis and peptic ulcer, where incidence rates cannot usefully be derived.

Both kinds of rates have in common that they are arithmetical fractions resspresenting the proportion of a population that is affected by a disease and thus they express the risk in that population of experiencing the disease or condition under consideration. As fractions, they represent a numerator divided by a denominator. The numerator is the number of cases of the disease, the denominator is the related population.

In the simplest cases, the choice of denominator with which to express the risk associated with a disease is quite obvious. For example, if we are studying the incidence of appendicitis in Britain in 1968 we need to know the number of cases of the disease during the year (the numerator) and the number in the population of Britain during the year (the denominator). Since the population changes during the year only very slightly, the average number, or the estimated mid-year number, of the population will do very well as denominator. But, to take a difficult example, the incidence of allergic diseases among seasonal hop-pickers presents a very different problem. Neither the numerator nor the denominator is easy to define or ascertain, and both will show marked seasonal fluctuations. The definition and ascertainment of numerators and denominators and the problems of their mutual appropriateness loom large among the methodological difficulties of social medicine enquiry.

Incidence and prevalence are related. The factor which relates them is disease duration. Prevalence is the arithmetical product of incidence and average duration provided that duration is expressed in appropriate time units. For example, if the daily incidence of a disease is 3 per 1,000 of the population and the average duration is 3 days, then the prevalence on any day is 9 per 1,000. It is easy to see why this is so; on any day, there will be sick, the 3 per 1,000 of the population who became sick on that day, the 3 per 1,000 who became sick the previous day and the 3 per 1,000 who became sick the day before that. If the annual, rather than the daily, incidence had been quoted, the relationship would still hold provided that the average duration were also expressed in units of one year. This is so, because the annual incidence is 365 times the daily incidence and the duration in years is 1/365 times the duration in days.

The use of this relationship is often very convenient when two of the variables are ascertainable but not the third. Provided that neither the incidence nor the duration of a disease are changing very much with the passage of time the relationship can be very useful. For example, if we know the number of new cases of leukaemia registered each year and the number of currently living cases on the register, we can calculate the average duration of life with this disease. Alternatively, if we know the average duration of life and the annual number of new cases we can calculate the number currently suffering from the disease. An application of this relationship occurs in the study of hospital utilization. Hospital admission rates (which are calculated from the number of admissions during a year divided by the number in the population served by the hospitals), are effectively incidence rates, while residence rates (number resident at a point in time divided by number in population) are prevalence rates. Average duration of hospital stay can be calculated if admission and residence rates are known. In fact, even if the population served by a hospital is difficult to define (as it often is), we can calculate the average duration of hospital stay, provided that we know the number of admissions during the year, the number of beds in the hospital and the average proportion of beds that are occupied at any time. This technique is often used to compare duration of stay in different hospitals and hospital wards. If average duration of stay is short and bed turnover time long, the method is unreliable, but for mental hospitals and hospitals for the chronic sick, it is very useful.

In relation to mortality statistics there are a number of standard rates that are very widely used. Mortality rates are generally calculated by dividing the number of deaths during a year by the number in the population at risk during the year. Thus, the number of deaths is the numerator and the number in the related population is the denominator. In most cases the procedures are simple, but since they are widely used and there are a number of anomalies in their method of calculation, it may be useful to consider them in more detail.

The crude death rate of a population, such as a national or other major complete population, is obtained by dividing the number of deaths in that population at the mid-year. Crude death rates are usually expressed as rates per 1,000 and vary among different countries from about 6 per 1,000 to about 12 per 1,000.

There are a number of problems in the interpretation of death rates; some of these derive from the calculation methods and some from their use in comparative studies. Most of the problems are rather technical and need not detain us here since crude death rates are more used in demographic studies than in studies in social medicine. One problem is very important, however, because it has resulted in the development of more complex indices of mortality. This problem emerges when we examine crude death rates for different countries and for different regions within a country and find, as we do, that the rates do not seem to reflect what we should expect from our knowledge of the relative healthiness of the populations. For example, we frequently find that the highest rates occur in those areas we should expect to be healthy (e.g. the south coast of England) and the lowest rates in areas where we know that general conditions are least conducive to health (e.g. the industrial towns). The reasons for these anomalous findings lie in the age composition of the populations concerned. Whatever variation there may be between mortality in different places, it is generally small in relation to the variation that occurs among people of different ages. Mortality in the first few weeks of life is high; thereafter it falls sharply and remains low during childhood and adolescence; from then on mortality rises increasingly steeply with every year of age. A population that has a high proportion of older members will have a high crude death rate, while a population predominantly composed of young people will have a low crude death rate. The effect of marked differences in age composition will usually more than offset any differences due to environment. In general, the countries and regions where high standards of public health prevail will have enjoyed a lowered early mortality for long enough to have shifted the age composition of their population towards the older ages. Migration of retired people may augment the effect within a country. Areas with older populations will usually have high crude death rates. Countries with poor health standards often have a high birth rate and a high

early mortality; they usually have a young population, therefore, and a low crude death rate. If we wish to compare populations from the point of view of mortality, so that mortality
rates reflect the general levels of health, then it is obvious that
we shall need to devise an index which permits comparison of
the risk of death but takes into account differences in population age composition. The simplest solution is to compare
mortality in the various populations, but to restrict comparison
to comparable age levels in the population. To do this, we may
calculate age specific death rates in which, for each age, we
divide the number dying at that age by the number in the
population at that age. For practical purposes it suffices to
group ages into five or ten year intervals. The general practice
is to calculate death rates for persons under one year old, for
those aged 1 to 4 years, 5–9 years, 10–14 years and so on in
five year intervals until the age range 85 and over. In each case
the number of persons dying in the age range in question is
divided by the number in the population at that age and expressed as a rate per 1,000 or per 100,000. If we now wish to
compare two populations, we may compare each age specific
death rate in the two populations and we shall have taken
into account any differences between the populations in respect
of age composition.

This procedure is satisfactory if we wish to compare a small
number of populations. But if we wish to compare the mortality of a large number of populations the mass of figures
involved is more than can usefully be assimilated. Age specific
death rates are usually calculated separately for the two sexes
and if they are calculated for 19 different age groups there will
be 38 figures for each population being considered. If we wish
to compare mortality in all the nations of the world or in all
the boroughs in England then the data become impossibly
voluminous. What is evidently required is a simple figure for
each population which would summarize its mortality while
adjusting for differences in age composition.

It is easy to suggest a simple, if crude, method. If we averaged the specific mortality rates for the various ages and the
two sexes in each population we should have for each popula-

tion a figure which would be equivalent to the crude death rate for that population if the numbers in the population at each age were equal. Since the same assumption would be involved in each population for which the calculation were performed, the resulting average death rates would reflect differences in mortality but would correct for differences in age composition between the populations. In practice, the method is not used in this simple form. The reason is chiefly that a population with equal numbers in each age group is hardly ever encountered in reality and the procedure therefore gives an unrealistic figure for the individual population. However, a somewhat similar procedure has been used and is called the Equivalent Average Death Rate. This involves averaging the specific death rates for the two sexes and for the age groups 0–4, 5–9, 10–14 . . . 60–64, and omitting the rates for the older ages. The justification is that over the age range 0–64 in some countries the numbers in the population at each five year age range are not too grossly dissimilar.

However, the more usual procedure is to calculate some form of standardized death rate or mortality index. The best known and most widely used, as well as the most statistically sound of these indices is the Standardized Mortality Ratio or S.M.R. Calculation of the S.M.R. involves calculating for each population under comparison, the number of deaths that would occur in it if, at each age, it experienced the age specific death rates of a suitably chosen standard population. The actual number of deaths is then expressed as a percentage of this calculated number. This Ratio expresses the relative mortality experience of the real population compared with that in the standard population and corrects for differences in age composition between the real population and the standard. The method is greatly used for making comparisons of mortality in population groups having grossly dissimilar age compositions such as, for example, the workers in different industries or occupations. The principal difficulty in its use concerns the choice of a suitable set of standard rates. In occupational mortality comparisons it is common to use for this purpose the rates for all employed persons in the country or for all males in the country. These amount, more or less, to the aggregate of the individual populations being studied and such an aggregate is generally a good choice for a standard population. It is naturally necessary to use the same standard population for each of the populations under comparison.

The use of age standardized death rates greatly facilitates comparison of the mortality experience of different populations. These may be large national populations or identifiable sections of a large population. Mortality rates may be calculated for all causes of death or for individual causes. In later chapters we shall use S.M.R.s for a number of diseases as a means of comparing their occurrence among different groups in the community.

For international comparisons, other kinds of standardized mortality rates are often used. These all have in common that they relate the mortality experience within individual populations to that in a standard population in such a way as to take account of differences in age composition. However, for many simple purposes there are a number of other ways in which the relative healthiness of communities may be compared. Much the simplest general index of health is the infant mortality rate. Infant mortality is a sensitive index of general health conditions in a country and is relatively simple to calculate if the appropriate data are available. These are; the number of live births in the community during the year, and the number of deaths during the year of children aged less than one year. The infant mortality rate is obtained by dividing the number of such deaths by the number of live births and expressing the resulting fraction as a rate per 1,000 live births. Rates in various countries vary from around 15 per 1,000 to around 150 per 1,000. Most countries are able to obtain the requisite data for at least part of their populations.

A difficulty may arise if either the number of births or the number of infant deaths is changing in a population. This is because not all the deaths of children under one year of age occur to children born during the same calendar year as that in which they die. A sudden rise in the number of births in one year will cause an artificial lowering of the infant mortality rate for that year and if the rise in number of births is not sustained, may cause a rise in the infant mortality rate for the following year. However, in most cases these distortions are unimportant for two reasons. First, the numbers of births and deaths in most populations are reasonably stable from year to year. Second, in most populations, the majority of infant deaths occur early in the first year of life and thus most of them occur in the same calendar year as the births of the individuals involved. As we shall see later, in the developed countries, the crowding of infant deaths into the first few weeks or even days of life is particularly marked.

For many purposes, interest is centred on deaths in the first month of life. The rate which summarizes this early mortality is called the neonatal mortality rate and is calculated by dividing the number of deaths, in a calendar year of infants aged less than 28 days, by the number of living births in that year. The result is expressed as a rate per 1,000 live births. This rate is clearly much less subject than the infant mortality rate to vagaries arising from annual fluctuations in the number of births, since most neonatal deaths occur in the same calendar year as the births of the individuals involved.

Mortality in the remainder of the first year of life is expressed by the post-neonatal mortality rate. This is calculated by dividing the number of infants dying at ages between 28 days and one year, by the number of live births during the year. It is a most unsatisfactory rate since not all live born infants are at risk of dying in this period since some of them will already have died in the neonatal period. The rate is very little used for comparative studies. In developed countries it is generally very low and in other countries it may be difficult to obtain the necessary data for its calculation.

It is generally the case that mortality in the post-neonatal period is determined by causes operating in post-natal life whereas the causes of neonatal mortality are more often prenatal or intranatal. The lower the infant mortality rate the larger is the neonatal rate in relation to the post-neonatal rate and the less the neonatal mortality is determined by post-natal causes. This is because the improvements in the post-natal environment which have lowered post-neonatal mortality have not been matched by improvements in the prenatal environment which has remained relatively inaccessible to study or to control.

This recent concentration on prenatally determined mortality has naturally focused attention on prenatal death itself. This is expressed in the stillbirth rate, which is calculated as the number of stillbirths in a year divided by the sum of the numbers of live and stillbirths in that year and expressed as a rate per 1,000 total births.

There remains the considerable problem of defining a stillbirth. The internationally recommended definition defines a stillbirth as a foetus which is dead at birth and is born after the 28th week of pregnancy. Estimation of the duration of pregnancy is difficult and must usually be based on the mother's recollection of the date of her last menstrual period. In many countries, the formalities associated with registration of stillbirths are not enforced for dead foetuses born after less than 28 weeks of pregnancy and so there is considerable temptation to underestimate this duration in doubtful or borderline cases. This represents an important source of error in stillbirth rates. Even more important is the problem of defining death and of deciding whether it took place before or after birth. In many cases, the foetal death occurs during the process of birth and the decision may be difficult. Rules for deciding are difficult to formulate. The international definition describes a stillbirth as a child which 'after issuing from its mother did not breathe or show any sign of life . . .', and then proceeds to itemize a few such signs of life. Nevertheless, it is clear that interpretation of the rules is very variable. In addition, the variation is not random. In some countries, social security maternity payments are made only for live births; it is likely that in such countries signs of life will be diligently sought. In other countries, registration procedures are much simpler for stillbirths than for livebirths followed by early infant death; in such countries the search for signs of life may be less diligent. Religious and other cultural influences may also affect the decision between whether to regard a dead newborn child as liveborn or stillborn.

For these reasons, and also for the reason that the causes of death at and around birth are much the same whether the death occurs before, during or after birth, it is now usual to study perinatal mortality. The perinatal death rate does not yet have an official international definition but by general agreement it is calculated by adding the number of stillbirths and the number of deaths of infants aged less than one week and dividing by the sum of the number of stillbirths and the number of livebirths. The rate is usually expressed as a rate per 1,000 total births. Usually the perinatal deaths and the total births are taken from the events of the same calendar year but the consequent discrepancy between numerator and denominator is trivially small. Perinatal mortality is the subject of intensive study in many countries since it represents the residual early mortality that has remained relatively intractable during a period of otherwise quite spectacular reductions in the mortality of early life.

An index which is often employed in comparative studies of mortality is the expectation of life at birth. This index has been most misleadingly named. For a complete understanding of its meaning it is necessary to study the actuarial technique of the life table on which calculation of the expectation of life is based. In the present context a simple explanation of life table technique will be sufficient.

If we have calculated for a population at some point in time, the currently prevailing age specific death rates, their comparison with similar data for other populations may be unwieldy if the number of populations is large. As we have seen, this problem may be tackled by calculation of standardized rates but there are occasions when this technique summarizes the data more than is required. On such occasions the data may be summarized by means of a life table. This is simply a device which takes a hypothetical population of newborn individuals of a convenient and round-numbered size, and calculates the way in which such a population would diminish if it were subjected at each successive age to the age specific mortality of the real population that we wish to study. For example, if we assume 1,000 newborn individuals for our life-table population and the age specific death rate for the first five years of life is 30 per 1,000, then at the end of the first five years our original 1,000 would have been reduced to 970. If the age specific rate for the next five years is 10 per 1,000 then the number would be diminished by 970 × 10/1,000 = 9·7 and would be 961·3 at the end of ten years. Successive application of this procedure to the successive age periods of life will attenuate the hypothetical population towards zero. The pattern of attenuation may vary through the age span considered and may be illustrated graphically. Variation in the shape of the attenuation curves may illustrate important differences between the mortality experience of the populations on which they are based. It is important to remember, however, that the generations whose attenuation is being illustrated are hypothetical although the mortality rates that are attenuating them are usually those of a real population at a point in time. No real generation of individuals need exist, or ever have existed, whose attenuation through life at all resembles that of the life table population.

However, life tables have been used by actuaries to calculate the risks incurred by companies offering life insurance. It is obviously necessary for the quotation of competitive premium rates to have some idea of the likely disbursement of assured sums that may have to be made. Calculation of such risks involves making many assumptions and introducing a number of safeguards both of which may enormously complicate the calculation. For medical statistical purposes, where no predictive function need be served, the calculation of expectation of life may be much simpler. Essentially, the process consists of summing the total years of life lived by the hypothetical population and dividing by the number chosen as the starting population. Thus the expectation of life at birth represents the average number of years of life that would be lived by a hypothetical population if it experienced at each age of life, the mortality rates in a real population at a particular point in time. It has no predictive value whatsoever; it simply summarizes a population's current mortality experience in a way which may be helpful for some particular purposes. The expectation of life may be calculated beyond other points than birth. In such cases it represents the average number of years that would be lived beyond the particular age under consideration. The expectation naturally gets shorter as the age point chosen gets older but the sum of the age and the expectation beyond it gets progressively longer. This sum changes quite markedly between birth and the end of the first year of life since mortality in the first year of life is very much higher than in the succeeding years in most real populations.

We have raised, in the preceding paragraphs, a problem which is quite important in the study of age specific mortality in populations. If we use information on deaths occurring during a year, and on the population in which they occur, to calculate a set of age specific mortality rates, these age specific rates express the risk of death for people in that population, at each age during that *year*. Thus, the death rate at ages 45–49 expresses the risk of death during a year for a person in that age range and the rates at all the other ages express their age specific risks. But it is important to note that they relate to people at the ages in question during the year for which the rates were calculated. A similar set of rates calculated from data for a year fifty years earlier would likewise express the risk of death for people at the various ages during that earlier year. This may seem quite obvious, and indeed it is, but the difficulty arises when we wish to understand how the risk of death varies—perhaps for a particular disease—as human beings go through life. We cannot simply assume that the age specific death rates calculated for a particular year express the change in risk as life advances. For the people aged 45–49 this year belong to a different generation from those aged 5–9 during this year or from those aged 75 and over. When they were young and when they become old their risk of death may be quite different from the risks associated with young people or with old people at the present time. This is one reason why life tables can be misleading; they falsely seem to show the change in risk of death as life advances. The problem is important in relation to diseases arising from exposure to long continued influences and where successive generations may be experiencing a different intensity or duration of exposure. It is particularly important in lung cancer where neglecting to consider this problem has resulted in misleading conclusions being drawn (see chapter 8) and it has general importance for all studies concerned with the increasingly important question of the influence of age on disease incidence.

In fact, it is odd that the influence of age on disease has been relatively neglected. It has generally been taken for granted that as we get older we become more liable to disease or death, but the mechanism of this effect has only quite recently been studied and we still know very little about it. It seems likely to be a fruitful line of enquiry if we can solve some of the associated methodological problems. These arise principally from the difficulties of comparing data on disease occurrence over a period of time during which changes in diagnostic precision and fashion may have influenced the apparent disease experience of the populations under study.

In the analysis of large scale data, whether they relate to morbidity or to mortality, many problems arise from the need to classify the data in diagnostic and other terms. Whereas it is relatively easy to characterize the disease condition and other relevant features of an individual patient, it is much more difficult when we come to characterize a group of patients or a section or the whole of a population. The difficulty arises from the fact that no two people are exactly alike and no two cases of illness present exactly similar features. Nevertheless, the ordering of observations so that they may be characterized in groups and the characteristics of the groups examined, is a fundamental requirement of scientific investigation. In seeking to study the disease experience of groups of people we need to isolate the features possessed in common by those among them who become sick and to differentiate useful classes within the groups.

Diagnostic classification has been a preoccupation of medicine since its earliest times. Its main purpose has been to permit the recognition of instances where treatment may be based

on general experience of the course of similar illnesses encountered in the past, either by the physician himself or by
other physicians whose experience is available for guidance.
Clearly, if a disease may be given a suitable identification we
can choose a treatment that is known to have been effective
in similarly identified cases in the past. In this way, a doctor
who can consistently identify the diseases from which his
patients suffer, may successfully exploit the general therapeutic
experience of the profession even in cases of illness that he
may be encountering for the first time. This function of the
process of diagnosis is a practical one. The attachment of a
diagnostic label to the actual sickness suffered by the patient
serves as the basis for choosing an appropriate treatment. If
this were the only use of diagnosis we should need only as
many diagnostic categories as we have different remedies
available; the introduction of a universal antibiotic with a
constant dose schedule for all infections would abolish the
need to distinguish between different infections. In practice, of
course, such a universal treatment is unlikely to be introduced.
In addition, during the history of medicine, diagnosis has
come to serve a whole range of functions quite apart from
providing guidance in the treatment of individual patients.
For a large part of the history of medicine effective remedies
have not been available. The prevention of diseases has therefore been at least as interesting as their cure. Improvements in
both prevention and treatment have been considered as depend-
ing on our being able to intervene in a sequence of causally
related events comprising the onset, course and resolution of
disease. For these reasons, diagnosis has become oriented towards an understanding of aetiology and the diagnostic classification of sickness now tends to reflect disease causation.
Thus, diagnostic terminology has changed from a preoccupation with symptomatic description to a preoccupation with
causal relationships.

In social medicine, diagnostic classification serves a somewhat different function. First, it seeks to group together instances of sickness whose general importance is similar, and
second, it serves to group diseases in terms of a concept of

causation which leads to the possibility of intervention by socially based action. For example, cholera and typhoid fever have very little in common clinically or from the point of view of the pathogenic organisms involved, but they are both caused by drinking contaminated water and are therefore justifiably grouped as water-borne diseases and tackled preventively by virtually identical means. Similarly, cancer of the bladder and toxic jaundice are pathologically and therapeutically very dissimilar but they may both arise in consequence of exposure to industrial processes and therefore have similar social implications.

The problem in classifying diagnoses in data on population disease experience is that the available data usually derive from diagnoses made by clinicians and therefore based on a diagnostic terminology and classification that are appropriate for clinical rather than social medical purposes. To solve this problem, various statistical classifications of diseases have been proposed which take the diagnostic terms in current use in medical practice and classify them in a way which meets public health requirements while doing as little violence as possible to taxonomic concepts appropriate to the clinical origins of the data. Of these classifications the most generally accepted are the International Statistical Classification and the adaptation of it prepared by the United States Public Health Service. The International Statistical Classification of Diseases, Injuries and Causes of Death is sponsored by the World Health Organization whose members agree to use it for certain published data on morbidity and causes of death. In practice, its use is very much wider. The W.H.O. undertake its periodic revision at ten-year intervals to ensure that it continues to accommodate the diagnostic terms that are in current use and to reflect currently accepted notions on disease causation and the relationship between diseases. The decennial revisions are based on the advice of an Expert Committee which meets at intervals in the years between revisions and reviews proposals submitted to W.H.O. by the national committees of member states and by experts in the various relevant fields. Inevitably, the periodic revisions embody many compromises of conflicting views; few authorities will agree on the best basis for a disease classification and the different medical traditions of different countries and their different disease experiences lead to very different needs for classification. Nevertheless, the International Classification enjoys a very wide use which seems a reasonable testimony to its general acceptability.

The history of the International Classification affords an interesting example of early international co-operation in public health. Its beginnings were in a classification produced in 1893 by Jacques Bertillon of the city statistical department of Paris and presented to a meeting of the International Statistical Institute in Chicago. Bertillon's classification was based on a synthesis of classifications used in Britain, Germany and Switzerland. It was quite widely adopted in many countries and recommendations were made that it should be revised decennially. In 1900 the French Government called the first International Conference for the revision of Bertillon's classification and this was succeeded by revision conferences in 1910 and 1920 under Bertillon's guidance. In 1928 the Health Organization of the League of Nations published a study carried out by a Committee of Expert Statisticians and in consequence a 'Mixed Commission' was established of members from the International Statistical Institute and the League's Health Organization. This Commission was responsible for revisions in 1929 and 1938 which were called the Fourth and Fifth Revisions of the International List of Causes of Death.

Since that time, the scope of the classification has been expanded to deal with morbidity statistics, and more recently, so as to be adaptable for use as a diagnostic index. The Sixth revision was in 1948, the Seventh in 1955 and the Eighth in 1965, the decennial sequence having been disturbed by the second world war. The classification principle is eclectic and does not follow a consistent plan throughout. For example, it begins by grouping together the diseases that are caused by micro-organisms under the heading of Infective and Parasitic Diseases. Next, it groups together neoplasms which are then distinguished chiefly by anatomical site but partly by their microscopic structure and behaviour. Then it groups together a whole miscellaneous collection of allergic, endocrine and metabolic diseases; next, diseases of the blood. Then the axis of classification changes again to one based on the functional systems of the body—nervous system, circulatory system, respiratory system and so on. Groups are also included that are based on the age at which diseases occur; for example, congenital malformations, diseases of infancy and senile diseases. Finally there is a group of diseases due to violence which is labelled Accidents, Poisoning and Violence, and exists in two alternative forms, one based on the nature of the injury and one on the nature of the cause.

The International Classification is published by W.H.O. in two volumes; one contains the classification and the list of diagnoses to be included under each heading, while the other contains an index. It is important to recognize that this classification is not simply a list of diagnostic terms but a classification, that is to say, a grouping of all the currently used diagnostic terms into some 600 categories which are arranged in a meaningful hierarchical form and each of which has a name and a simple numerical code number. The latter facilitates the recording of diagnostic categories on the punched cards that are used in computers and other statistical data processing machines used in analysis of population data on disease.

Although classification of disease now has a widely accepted international basis, the classification of other relevant attributes of patients is less well developed. By common consent, and for clear reasons, patients are usually classified by sex and age in most studies of population disease experience. But there are other important personal attributes which need to be examined. In Britain, the Registrar General for England and Wales has prepared a Classification of Occupations and an associated classification of social class. The classification of occupations has functions which parallel those of the International Classification of Diseases; they are to reduce the enormous range of individually different occupations to a list of manageable size in which the listed categories are individually reasonably homogeneous and usefully distinct from one another. Occupation has an important bearing on disease experience and it is useful to have a manageable classification.

The Registrar General's social classes have a considerable celebrity, if not notoriety. They were introduced as a convenient means of dividing the population into five groups distinguished by their social standing in so far as it relates to health. They are simply based on occupation; each occupation being assignable to one of the five social classes, which are denoted by the roman numerals I to V. The classes may be summarized as follows:

I. Professional and Managerial occupations,
II. Intermediate between I and III,
III. Skilled occupations; mainly manual,
IV. Partly skilled occupations; mainly manual,
V. Unskilled occupations.

Married women are usually assigned to the class of their husband's occupation and children to the class of the occupation of their father or the head of their family.

At the time of its introduction, this system was intended to distinguish five classes which were distinct not only in their occupational background but also in their educational and general social standing. The intention was to use the classes as a simple means of demonstrating important differences in the disease experience of different sections of the population, distinguished by their general economic, educational and social environment. To some extent, such demonstrations involve a circular argument since the original classification was partly determined by different morbidity experiences. But the utility of the system must be regarded as vindicated by its productivity in terms of the useful hypotheses that have proceeded from its use and which have underlain many important advances in medicine. It seems likely that its useful life may now be nearly over and that a more critical classification of social characteristics is required. That no adequate successor has yet been found testifies not only to the difficulty of proposing a better method but also to the simplicity and effectiveness of the present one.

In this chapter we have touched on some of the methods and problems of large scale analysis of data on population disease experience. Most of the methods have been developed over a period when available data processing resources were relatively crude and simple. The future is dominated at present by expectations of an enormously enhanced facility for statistical analysis arising from the use of electronic computers. Present methods will almost certainly continue to play a substantial role in the next decade or so.

Chapter 4 Special surveys

Many of the problems which engage the attention of research workers in social medicine are studied by means of smaller-scale studies than those we have considered so far. A small-scale study may be chosen either because the available data are not more numerous or because the detail required precludes their collection and analysis on a larger scale. The smaller-scale study may be thought of as analogous to the use of microscopic examination in which the details are examined closely after the whole has been surveyed on a broader scale. For example, a large scale examination[4] of the functioning of the maternity services has indicated that mothers who particularly require hospital delivery are frequently delivered at home, despite the availability of hospital accommodation. Further investigation of the problem will almost certainly necessitate the detailed investigation of a small representative series of maternities to ascertain the reasons for the non-utilization of available maternity care. It would usually be quite impracticable to carry out such an investigation on the large population scale. On other occasions the use of small-scale data may be indicated by the basic nature of the problem. For example, we may wish to study the natural history of a relatively rare disease or to investigate a limited outbreak. In such cases, detailed investigation may be made of all occurring cases of the condition being studied.

Much the most usual situation in social medicine research is that a small-scale study is planned because of the need for detailed information; it is usually the case that the small series of observations will be used to draw inferences about the much larger population of cases of whom the small series may be assumed to be representative. This is a feature of the greater part of scientific investigation. Research is usually planned in such a way that conclusions based on a necessarily limited actual range of observations may legitimately be generalized into statements having force beyond the actual realm of the observations. This involves three principal obligations. The first is that the observational situation must be devised so as to avoid the possible effects of purely localized influences which may affect the issue. The second is that observations must be communicated to other research workers so that crucial observations may be repeated—if necessary, in different circumstances. The third obligation is that all hypotheses must be recognized as provisional and be susceptible of being tested, modified or discarded if subsequent observations indicate that any of these courses may be desirable.

In a study that is based on a relatively small series of observations, the problem of their general representativeness is paramount. It is also often extremely difficult. We are frequently in the position that we can only guess at what circumstances may be relevant and we are therefore frequently in the position of being wrong in our guesses. This is true for all scientific enquiry. For research to be reasonably productive it must be conceived and carried out by investigators who are well informed about the subject matter of the investigation and who have experience of, and insight into, the likely problems involved in a particular field of enquiry. It is a problem for all new sciences or for sciences which may be rapidly expanding that the available background of experience and knowledge may be quite limited. If, as has been suggested, scientific enquiry is an art, it is one in which a good apprenticeship is invaluable whatever the innate gifts of the artist.

The problem of representativeness may arise before or after the observations have been made. There are many occasions when the observational situation cannot be designed in advance since the occurrence of the phenomena to be observed cannot be arranged. For example, investigation of the origin and mode of transmission of a smallpox outbreak consists generally of interpretation of observations forced upon our attention by the occurrence of the outbreak. If we are to use such data in order to draw conclusions concerning smallpox in general, it is necessary to consider carefully the respects in which the observed cases may not be representative of all cases. It would rarely be practicable to arrange in advance to make observations on so rare and spasmodic a disease. A similar situation arises when a disease occurs sufficiently uncommonly to make it desirable to assemble data on a series of cases that have already occurred. Such a retrospective collection of data poses a number of interpretative problems.

It seems appropriate at this point to discuss the general question of the desirability of retrospective enquiries. Examples of such enquiries will be discussed frequently later in this book. It is often assumed that data obtained retrospectively are seriously suspect and should hardly ever form the basis for any but the most tentative hypothesis. The danger of this attitude, which is basically the healthy one that all hypotheses are suspect in scientific enquiry, is that all too often it leads to an uncritical acceptance of hypotheses based on non-retrospective data, particularly if they contradict a retrospectively based one. An example of this, which will be discussed in detail later, was the rejection of the quite soundly based view that prenatal exposure to diagnostic X-rays may predispose a child to the development of leukaemia in post-natal life. The original work was based, for very good reasons, on retrospective data on X-irradiation. It seems worth asserting that, since we are confronted by a world which is very difficult to understand, we should neglect no means that may be at our disposal for furthering our understanding, providing that we always observe the sound rule of considering very carefully the possibility of interpretations of our data other than the one we choose.

Perhaps the best way to achieve representative data on any phenomena of which we can observe only a proportion, is to make our observations on a randomly drawn sample. The theory and practice of sampling are very complex matters which are outside the scope of the present work but it may be helpful to outline some of their applications to social medical enquiry. The general question may best be illustrated by examples.

Suppose that we wish to discover what are the principal diseases for which people are admitted to hospital and for how long they necessitate staying in hospital. In many countries it would be quite impracticable to take a census of all hospital patients or to examine case records for all discharges. We might therefore decide to study a representative fraction of all patients in hospital. Since we wish to know how long patients stay in hospital it will be necessary in practice to take our sample from all patients discharged from hospital. It might be relatively simple to keep suitable records of diagnosis and duration of stay for all the patients for a single hospital for a month. But we are immediately faced with the questions of which hospital to select and which month. It seems very likely that hospitals vary in the kinds of diseases that they treat and that the months of the year vary since several common diseases show a seasonal variation in occurrence. Can we select a representative hospital and a representative month? This may be possible but does not seem very likely. In any case, how shall we know that the hospital and the month that we select are representative? We may attempt such a selection and make our study, but we shall need to qualify our conclusions so considerably that we may end by being relatively little the wiser for a considerable expenditure of effort in the investigation. Nevertheless, it may well be that any information at all might represent a worthwhile improvement on what we already know, and it may be impossible to select a better sample. It is, in fact, frequently necessary to depend on information whose representativeness may be in doubt but which may be the only information available for examination. For example, we have frequently to judge the merits of a new surgical procedure on the basis of the experience of a single surgeon who has developed it. We are often unable to assess its likely success in other hands or on another series of patients. Although we may design an efficient evaluation procedure for early implementation there is nearly always a stage at which we must take a decision of some sort on the available data. It is important to recognize that wrong decisions may have just as serious consequences whether they are positive or negative. If we decline to accept a new treatment as worthy of trial we may be delaying the development of worthwhile advances. If we accept the new treatment we may be exposing patients to danger as well as unnecessarily discarding a worthwhile existing treatment.

To return to the example of the study of diagnosis and duration of stay for hospital patients; although we may have to select what we hope are representative data, it is obviously better to attempt to ensure their representativeness. In order to deal with the problem of seasonal variation it would be best to attempt to cover the whole year in the collection of data. If daily collection throughout the year involves too much labour we might consider taking hospital discharges on several days of each month. It is important to avoid choosing days which may be popular ones for discharging patients since this may bias the sample in the direction of including too many patients whose illnesses permit the selection of a suitable day for discharge. If the selected days cover the month fairly well (for example every third day) such a procedure should meet the case. It may be important in some cases to avoid taking the same number of days for each month since, in fact, the months vary in their length and a sample which took the same number of days for each month would cause over-representation of the short months. It is often more practical to take a sample of patients rather than of months or days. This can be achieved, for example, by taking every tenth patient, or every third or every twentieth throughout the year. Again, it may be important to avoid certain fractions. For example, if we took every 100th patient then the small hospitals might either go unrepresented if they admitted fewer than one hundred patients or might always contribute their autumn or winter patients if their admissions just exceeded one hundred in the year.

The selection of representative hospitals might be achieved either by selecting the hospitals on some suitably random basis or by selecting patients in a random way and assuming that they will be randomly distributed among the hospitals. A simple procedure for selecting an essentially random collection of patients is to choose patients born on particular days of the year. There are obvious precautions to be observed if the patients may include newborn infants whose characteristic diseases often show a sharp seasonal pattern. A possible solution to the problem of selecting a small random sample of patients might be to select all patients whose birthday fell on the first day of any month. Possible complications of such a procedure might arise if knowledge of a patient's date of birth and therefore of his inclusion in the sample might influence the recording of diagnosis or the timing of his discharge.

The foregoing discussion illustrates a number of the problems involved in sampling. Although a detailed discussion is outside the scope of the present work, it may be useful to consider the question a little more generally.

Random or quasi-random sampling involves the selection of a sample in such a way that nothing other than chance materially determines which individuals are included in the sample and which left out. The concept of chance is a difficult one; chance events may be defined as events that are due to a multiplicity of indeterminate causes. In practical situations it is usually sufficient that the method of selection cannot conceivably influence any findings based upon the data. Thus, if we collect data on hospital patients whose dates of birth are the 5th, 15th and 25th of the month they should represent a random 10 per cent sample from the point of view of an investigation into the sources of referral and disposal on discharge of hospital patients.

The principal problem which confronts the investigator is that of defining the population that he wishes to sample and listing them in a form appropriate to the sampling method he intends to employ. For example, in a study of the attitudes of the citizens of a town to the question of whether water supplies should be fluoridated, we might wish to obtain answers to a set of questions from a representative sample of the population. If we confined our attention to adults defined as over the age of twenty-one years, we might use the electoral roll as a frame from which to draw a suitable sample. This is a commonly employed device and has much to recommend it. But if we felt that we needed to question children or young adults as well, we should find it much more difficult. Studies of the smoking habits of children are of great public health interest but are rendered difficult by the absence of a suitable sampling frame. School registers may be helpful if we are content to restrict our investigation to persons under fifteen years but the diversity of types of school encountered in Britain and their often vague catchment areas may complicate the issue. If young adults in the age range 15 to 18 years are of interest, as in the case of smoking habits they would usually be, the problem of obtaining a random sample may be practically insuperable. This is why most studies of this question have been based on particular schools or groups of schools and their conclusions are consequently subject to qualification.

The choice of a sampling method clearly depends on the availability of suitable sampling frames as well as on the requirements of the investigation. Samples are therefore frequently used that are far from ideal but which are the best that may be available for the purpose. Use of such samples may be defended in terms of the proverbial injunction not to make the best the enemy of the good. Too great a straining after meticulously appropriate data may often involve one in abandoning an investigation which would have been quite valuable if carried out to less stringent criteria of investigational design.

A very great deal of social medical investigation as well as other scientific research is carried out on data which the investigator judges to be adequately representative for his purpose. In social medicine, which is concerned with populations, it is often impracticable to do other than confine an enquiry to the locality in which the investigator works. For example, epidemiological research into the causes of congenital malformations or chronic bronchitis have often been conducted within the confines of a city or other area to which the investigator has access. The conclusions are usually expected to have validity beyond this restricted domain. Such generalization of conclusions involves the need to consider the representativeness of the population being studied and it is usually, and probably justifiably, believed that such selection of data need not invalidate the conclusions that are drawn provided that due consideration is given to this problem. For example, a study of heart disease that is proceeding among the population of Framingham, Massachusetts, is generally conceded to be yielding data whose validity is of much wider application than the actual geographical area of the enquiry.

If a population can legitimately be selected as adequately representative for the purpose of the enquiries that are projected, it is often of great interest to establish within the selected population the total incidence or prevalence of a disease or other condition. A number of such total population studies have been of great interest. In Birmingham for several years, a study has sought to identify all cases of congenital malformations occurring among births in that city.[5] A long series of this kind, for which much aetiological relevant data are also available, is far more representative of all malformations than are series based on the aggregated experience of hospital births which are necessarily unrepresentative of all births with respect to such important variable as mother's age, birth order, and the incidence of obstetric complications. Prevalence studies in defined communities have also been of very great interest. Sometimes these have sought to examine the entire population of an area for signs of a particular disease; sometimes the whole spectrum of diseases within a community has been under study. The study of the Rhonda Valley being carried out by Cochrane and his colleagues[6] is an example. Virtually the whole population of the area has been examined and the occurrence of a wide variety of different disease conditions has been recorded.

Prevalence studies are particularly valuable where a chronic disease is under consideration whose onset is insidious and where it is not easy to define the diseased state. Chronic bronchitis is an example of a disease whose onset is indeterminate and where no natural simple criteria exist whereby cases may be admitted to or excluded from consideration. Tolerance of respiratory disability varies widely from person to person and consistent differences occur between different social and regional groups. Fletcher[7] has devised and validated a standard questionnaire on respiratory symptoms which consistently identifies a group of patients whose symptoms may be considered as defining chronic bronchitis. The development of such a questionnaire demands that the diseases can be validly, consistently and discriminately defined in terms of the symptoms that the questionnaire elicits. Fletcher's questionnaire has been published by the Medical Research Council and recordings are available which demonstrate its correct use. Its author has pointed out that the definition of diagnostic categories in social medical enquiry serves a different purpose from that involved in medical practice since in the latter we seek to avoid all error while in the former we seek simply to err consistently if at all.

An example of the use of the questionnaire on bronchitis in a total prevalence survey has been reported by Higgins[8] who used it to carry out a community survey in the town of Stavely in Derbyshire. This survey aimed at comparing the prevalence of bronchitis among foundry workers and men of similar age and domicile who had never worked in foundries. Comparisons were also made between men and their wives as well as comparisons aimed at comparing questionnaire methods with measurements of pulmonary function.

This method, which has proved so successful in the case of bronchitis, has yet to be employed on an important scale in the investigation of other largely symptomatic diseases. There is a particular need for similar methods in the study of mental illness.

There are many important problems of disease definition even in diseases where the diagnosis is not so heavily dependent on symptoms. Most clinicians adopt the attitude that the diagnostic terms they use have general meaning and that the same name always implies the same disease when the diagnoses have been made by competent clinicians. Clinical practice rarely affords an opportunity for verification of this assumption and since diagnosis in clinical medicine serves mainly the function of guiding the individual physician concerning how best to treat his patients, the assumption is usually unimportant. In social medicine enquiry, it often becomes important to be able to compare the disease experience of groups served by different physicians or to compare the findings of different investigators. It soon becomes apparent that consistency of diagnosis can often be achieved only by the adoption of the most rigorous diagnostic criteria. Even apparently simple physical signs of disease turn out to be inconsistently recorded. A recent investigation of the surgical treatment of breast cancer was an occasion for the discovery that experienced surgeons cannot agree about the presence of axillary lymph gland involvement—a sign which crucially determines a basic classification of disease severity on which choice of treatment often depends. On many occasions, the need for diagnostic consistency can only be satisfied by employing a single diagnostician for all examinations, or by arranging parallel examinations of the same patients so as to monitor the diagnostic standards and criteria that are employed.

But there are many diseases and disease conditions which are virtually impossible to define since they consist simply of extreme manifestations of characteristics common to all people. Hypertension is such a disease. The arterial blood of all living people is under pressure and in all healthy people the pressure may be measured by suitable techniques. Among healthy people the pressure of the arterial circulation varies; it may vary from day to day or from minute to minute in the same person, and variation between persons may be marked. There is a consistent tendency to find higher pressures among older people. It is also well recognized that among some people with higher than usual arterial pressures, a number of complications may arise which may lead to progressive organ damage, disability and eventual premature death. Where a raised pressure is associated with organ damage, or where the clinician judges that it may become so associated, the person is said to suffer from hypertension but there is no distinction to be made between hypertension and normal blood pressure on the basis of the actual level of the arterial pressure itself. Thus the study of abnormally high arterial pressure is not possible since no suitable basis exists for classifying pressures as abnormal. The study of hypertension resolves into the study of the determinants of the levels of arterial pressure and such studies involve the collection of data on arterial pressures among a representative sample of the population.

Many graded human characteristics resemble arterial pressure in that extreme degrees may be associated with disability or impaired survival to an extent which warrants their characterization as disease conditions. Height, intelligence, red blood cell count, rate of growth and weight at birth are all variable quantitative characteristics for which an extreme value in an individual constitutes a disease state. The distinction between normality and disease is in no case easy to draw and many of the distinctions drawn in clinical practice may be unjustifiably arbitrary in that they imply simple qualitative distinctions between health and disease. Studies of these characteristics may need to be made on representative populations in which individual values may be measured and related to aetiologically relevant variables.

Many studies in social medicine do not seek to identify individuals as suffering from particular diseases or conditions. Studies of the utilization of medical care or of public attitudes relevant to health may seek simply to explore the relationships between the various relevant attributes of members of a population. For example, we may wish to investigate the uptake of immunization against poliomyelitis or diphtheria in order to discover the influences which may affect the prevailing levels of immunization in a community. An important study[9] of poliomyelitis immunization has defined the groups within the population that have a relatively low uptake and who consequently require special attention in a population which is seeking to establish general protection against this disease. Another important study[10] has examined the associations between various characteristics of women and their utilization of available services for exfoliative cytological examination for the detection of early cancer of the uterine cervix. It has shown that those women who are most at risk of contracting this disease are least likely to avail themselves of the service aimed at its early detection. In such studies, small populations are examined, not for their disease experience but for characteristics of particular interest in the prevention of disease.

Social medicine concerns itself too with the functioning of

the institutions which may affect public health. The medical or nursing professions themselves may be studied, or their practices or training programmes. A study[11] undertaken by the Bureau of Applied Social Research in Columbia University has explored the processes underlying physicians' adoption of newly marketed drugs. The functioning of particular services (e.g. those for the chronic sick or laboratory services for general practitioners) have frequently been the subject of studies. Such studies usually involve selected samples rather than purely random samples since analysis of the functioning of an institution usually depends on the study of an intact integral unit. Thus, a particular hospital or set of hospitals within a community may be studied in respect of how it meets the community's needs for hospital care. Or a particular hospital ward may be studied so as to identify the roles of the various medical, nursing and other personnel concerned and to study how their interaction affects the quality of the care that patients receive.

The choice of a data recording and collection procedure reflects, therefore, the nature of the hypothesis it is proposed to investigate. Similarly, the selection of variables that are to be recorded will be governed by the nature of the problem as well as by what is available or recordable. It is often necessary in social medicine, as in other sciences, to develop new methods for obtaining the data that are needed for advancing knowledge of a particular subject. Examples of such new methods will frequently emerge in the later part of the present work and it will suffice here simply to draw attention to this aspect of field enquiry. It is frequently necessary to study variables which may be indicators of processes which it is still impossible to study in more detail. This is common in other sciences; for example, radiation from radioactive isotopes is commonly employed to 'trace' substances which may be involved in complex biological processes. Such use implies a confidence based on experience that the presence of the trace element is the most likely explanation of the observed radiation. Sociological 'trace elements' similarly aim at indicating the presence of processes which cannot be defined in detail. For example, the age at which individuals complete their whole-time education may permit the distinction of groups of persons in whom outlook and education differ and we may interpret differences in their disease experience or use of medical or health care accordingly. As in the use of radio-active isotopes, investigators should examine very carefully the implications of such indicators and should generally use them only when their experience of their use and of the systems they are studying warrants the act of confidence that is implied.

Since social medicine is concerned with the study of communities rather than of individuals, the variables that are recorded are usually ones which may be used to categorize groups. They may be quantitative or qualitative since group characterization may be by means of numerical properties or by means of the characteristic distribution of individuals into definable classes. Thus, we might compare two populations according to their average age and age range or by the relative proportions in them which may be classified as school children, economically active, or retired. The recording of the variables that are selected for examination will usually be either in numerical terms or by means of allocation to one of a set of exclusive and exhaustive categories. The choice of categories or of numerical units will be dictated by the purposes of the enquiry. It is generally extremely difficult to study variables which do not lend themselves either to measurement or to classification and much of the methodological difficulty of social medical enquiry arises from the need to devise useful indices which can be so handled. An example, which we have already mentioned, is social class; but in many studies of this problem the Registrar General's Classification is too crude and ambiguous. The classification of attitudes and expectations in relation to health, which may be necessary in studies of the use of medical and health services is often particularly difficult. In such cases, social medicine frequently needs to borrow methods from sister disciplines among the behavioural sciences.

Although much of the data used in social medical enquiry

may be objectively obtained by means of observation, much of it has to be obtained by interrogation of individuals. We have already discussed the case of the standard questionnaire on respiratory symptoms but there are, of course, many kinds of information which we may need to record which has not previously been the subject of special inquiry. Many items of information are relatively easy to obtain by interview with the subjects of an enquiry. For example, no serious errors or inconsistencies are usually involved in obtaining simple information on people's age, sex, marital status, or even occupation, although not even these items can be expected to be wholly reliably recorded. When more complex data are required, which may tax the memory of the subject or his understanding, considerable difficulties may be encountered. When there may be reasons why subjects might falsify information, either consciously or otherwise, particular care is required in obtaining the data and checks of the validity of information may need to be included. There is much experience of these problems among workers in the other behavioural sciences (psychology, sociology) but workers in social medicine are still often very naive in their approach. Nevertheless, much useful data has been recorded by interview and provided that caution is exercised in their interpretation useful hypotheses may often be founded on simple data. Many studies of nutrition, for example, have relied heavily on data recorded from the subjects by structured or partially structured interviews.

Analysis of field data presents a multiplicity of problems. Generally, analysis of social medical data is statistical, since we are concerned to characterize groups in terms of attributes which are variable among human populations and since we need to assess the significance of differences between groups and to draw inferences from samples concerning the populations that are sampled. It is obviously quite inappropriate in the present context to attempt a survey of the statistical methods in use in social medicine. The reader who wishes to know more of such methods must be referred to a text book of statistical methods—perhaps particularly, a book dealing with their application to the social or biological sciences. It will be sufficient to summarize the scope of the statistical method by defining it as concerned with the proper collection, analysis and interpretation of data on characteristics which may vary between individuals and in respect of which we need to collect and interpret small or large numbers of observations. Development of the science of statistics is mathematical; application of statistical methods to data involves arithmetical operations upon the data. The arithmetic may be relatively simple or it may be complex and laborious. In the past, statisticians have frequently been concerned with the development of analytical methods which involve a reasonably limited computational labour but which maintain an adequate degree of rigour and suitability. The introduction of fast electronic computing machines has transformed the task of analysing social medicine data as it has so many computational tasks in other fields. It is often now possible to employ more powerful methods than formerly since methods which were once prohibitively laborious may now require relatively trivial amounts of time on electronic computers.

Electronic computers also promise to revolutionize another aspect of social medicine enquiry. This is the assembly of data. For many purposes, social medical investigation may require the assembly of data that has already been placed on record in the process of documenting the practice of medicine. For example, we may need to assemble a series of cases of a particular disease or a set of patients having a particular set of characteristics. Since the practice of medicine involves quite extensive use of written records and written communications concerning patients, it is often possible to assemble a suitable series of observations from clinical records, case notes and laboratory reports. In particular, studies of the natural history of diseases have often been based on the analysis of such records. The classic work of Ellis[12] on nephritis involved the use of his own case records and the analysis of quite simple data by quite simple means yielded an important advance in medicine. As we shall see later, analysis of simple data from maternity records enabled McKeown and his colleagues in

Birmingham to explore the influences that determine the rate of foetal growth and the onset of labour in human pregnancy. If due regard is paid to questions of representativeness and to the possibility of incomplete or distorted recording, such data may be very valuable. However, although early work required little more than research intuition, clerical labour and simple arithmetic, most of the problems for which such data could now be used require a larger volume of information and much more complex analytical procedures. The increasing use of electronic computers for medical record-keeping will bring new possibilities to the use of such records by making it possible to recover more detailed data on a much larger scale and to analyse it more or less simultaneously.

This use of computers for automated record-keeping is currently the subject of intensive development. Suitable summaries are usually prepared of case notes and of laboratory reports from hospital patients. The summaries are stored in the filing system of a computer from where they may be retrieved very rapidly when wanted. Identified individual records may be retrieved, or specified categories of records may be assembled. In some applications the file may be effectively interrogated by the use of suitable computer programs. If developments can succeed in facilitating a more complete and reliable recording system as well as procedures for cross-referencing entries and carrying out analyses of selected records, we shall have a powerful new tool for social medical research.

Part II Areas of current enquiry

Chapter 5   Present and future problems in community health

Now that we have outlined the history of the development of social medicine and have indicated the range of its characteristic investigational techniques, we must consider the subject matter which social medicine is concerned to investigate. The current range of medical problems as they are encountered in all the countries of the world embraces an enormous scope. The relevant diseases range from the infective and nutritional disorders of the developing countries to the tumours and degenerative diseases of the West, and medical care problems range from those where there is one doctor to every 100,000 or more of the population to those where there is one doctor to every few hundred persons. The present writer's main experience has been in Britain where the problems are generally typical of those in Western temperate countries. Without in any way claiming that they are more widely representative than that, the writer proposes to consider particularly the medical problems of British society and to refer to the problems of other societies only in passing.

An understanding of the range of current medical problems that we are encountering in Britain and of those that we are likely to encounter during the next few decades, is best acquired by consideration of how the present situation arose. In the past century or so, the health condition of the British population has changed radically. Not all the changes are easy to identify and the details are sometimes particularly difficult to examine, but the changes that have principally brought about the present situation may be briefly summarized. The size of the population has changed; the age composition of the population has changed; the characteristic pattern of prevalent diseases has changed; and the structure and administration of the health and medical services has changed.

These changes are not equally easy to chart. Population changes may be studied from the reports of the Censuses which have been carried out in England and Wales since 1801 and in Scotland since 1841. It is possible from these reports to examine the overall changes, the regional changes and the changes in the age and sex distribution. The extent to which these changes have been effected by changes in birth and death rates may be studied from the annual reports of the Registrars General. The history of changes in the provision and administration of health services is well documented in the social and economic histories of the period and in the records of Parliament and of the responsible agencies. What is difficult to chart is the changing population experience of disease.

For these reasons, it may be well to leave until later the question of changes in disease patterns and to begin with the question of population change. The size of the British population has been increasing ever since any useable data have been available. We do not have wholly reliable figures for the period before the first Census in 1801 but there is little doubt that it had been growing since considerably before that date. In 1801 the population of England and Wales was just under 9 million, and it has since grown to some 46 million. It is generally accepted that the rate of growth began to increase before 1801 and most authorities believe that an acceleration in population growth occurred at around the beginning of the eighteenth century.

The lack of wholly reliable data for the earlier period has led to much speculation concerning the cause of the change in population growth. The controversy continues unresolved but its main features are interesting since they raise the important question of the relation of disease experience to population growth as well as the question of what precipitates disease changes which may influence population size. Since population size and the problems of supplying nutritional needs are very large among the problems of a great part of the world, the study of the antecedents of the current situation in Britain may be especially interesting.

A population will grow if its net gains exceed its net losses. If migration is not a major factor, population growth will occur if the birth rate exceeds the death rate and changes will occur in growth rates if the balance between birth and death rates become disturbed. There are thus three possible explanations of the population growth acceleration in eighteenth-century Britain. They are: that the birth rate rose; that the death rate fell; or that both eventualities occurred. Only the first two explanations have attracted a large following. The controversy was originally between those who argued that the rise was brought about by advances in medicine which greatly reduced the death rate and those who pointed out that the actual medical advances were not capable of having wrought such an effect and who consequently preferred the explanation of a rising birth rate. The question has been further complicated by McKeown[13] and his colleagues who agree that medical advances were probably unimportant but nevertheless believe that the rise was due to a falling death rate. Since adequate data do not exist on which a firm conclusion might be based, we have to reach any conclusion we may wish to draw from a consideration of the relative plausibility of the different possibilities. Most authorities agree that before the beginning of the eighteenth century the birth and death rates were both high. It would thus be easier for the death rate to fall than for the birth rate to rise. As McKeown has pointed out, a rising birth rate would have increased the average size of families and would probably have been largely offset by the high infant mortality which would have prevailed among the later children of large families. There are no grounds for supposing that the proportion of marriages that are fertile could have been raised appreciably by a possible tendency to earlier marriage. It is of interest in this context that data from the recent (1961) census show that the proportion of infertile marriages is not greatly affected by age at marriage; the only marked effect of a lowered age at marriage is to increase family size among fertile couples. The death rate has fallen fairly steadily since data have been available and it may plausibly be argued that it may have been falling for about a hundred years before that. McKeown dismisses medical advances as a cause of the falling death rate mainly on the grounds that the advances in question were of a kind more likely to interest doctors than to save patients and that, on the contrary, some of the surgical and obstetric advances of the time might well have adversely affected the survival of patients. He also pointed out that much of the improvement in mortality during the nineteenth century was due to a falling mortality from tuberculosis which cannot have been appreciably affected by treatment until comparatively modern times. It may be argued that McKeown's thesis depends unduly on a view of medicine as a specifically curative activity practised on individual patients and that it leaves out of account the possible influences of an improving medical and sanitary outlook on the general healthiness of the environment. It nevertheless seems reasonable to the present author to conclude that a falling death rate accounts for a large part of the population increase and that it was probably a feature of demographic trends among the developing nations of the west for at least two centuries.

It is also clear that a large part of the fall in death rates that undoubtedly took place in the nineteenth century was attributable to a decline in mortality from infectious disease. In the case of tuberculosis, which accounted for almost half of the fall, the causes are difficult to determine. It seems generally unlikely that changes in human immunity could be responsible since we have no evidence that such changes can occur on the scale required. Improvements in the housing environment can hardly have been the cause at a time when the mass of population movement was into the newly developing towns and cities. We are largely left with the likelihood that improvements in diet were the most important factor, a kind of neo-Malthusian view that a population's size is dependent on its available food supply.

Changes in the age and sex patterns of the population have accompanied the changes in overall size. During the period for which we have fully reliable data, the birth rate has remained higher than the death rate and, in the past one hundred years, both have fallen. This has had the effect that the population has grown steadily older. The female population has aged more than the male—a consequence of the more marked fall in the female death rate which has occurred while the birth rates for the two sexes have behaved similarly. These changes in the age and sex composition would naturally have affected the pattern of disease occurrence even if no other changes had occurred, since the characteristic diseases experienced by people of different ages differ very markedly.

That there have been substantial changes in the patterns of disease prevalence in Britain during the past one hundred years will be evident to anyone familiar with the fiction of the period. Tuberculosis, now a rare disease, was formerly widely prevalent, and diseases such as cholera, now thought of as rare and exotic, constituted a real and present menace at the mid-point of the last century. Death in childbirth, and the crippling bone infections of childhood were as commonplace to the Victorian novelists as are emotional maladjustment and neurotic depression to those of the present day. Even when allowance is made for the possibly unrepresentative sampling to which novelists may be prone, it is clear that the picture has changed. The precise nature of the changes and the emergence of the present pattern are somewhat more difficult to chart but the attempt to chart them is instructive, since it helps to explain the present situation and the problems we may have to face in the next few decades.

The difficulty of a historical analysis of disease occurrence stems both from the absence of data referable to the earlier period and from the difficulty of regarding as comparable such data as may be available. Fashions in diagnostic terminology are notoriously inconstant even over a short period of time; over a hundred years it is very difficult to compare data on individual diagnoses.

Nevertheless, the changes have been very striking. Table 5.1 shows the leading causes of death in Scotland in 1861 and 1961. The picture has changed so much that it seems quite impossible that the change can have been to more than a small extent due to changes in the content of diagnostic categories or to changes in the fashion or techniques of diagnosis. The infectious diseases were relatively well defined in 1861 and their characteristic mode of onset and course seem unlikely to have been confused with those which characterize the degenerative

Table 5.1

The leading causes of death in Scotland in 1861 and 1961. (From the relevant reports of the Registrar General)

1861	1961
1. Tuberculosis	Heart disease
2. Old age	Cancer
3. Bronchitis	Disease of cerebral arteries (haemorrhage and thrombosis)
4. Debility, premature birth and atrophy	Violence
5. Typhus	Bronchitis
6. Heart disease	Pneumonia
7. Whooping cough	Congenital malformations

The terms used in the table are the equivalent of those used in the actual statistical publications.

and neoplastic diseases. The relative changes in the importance of these groups of disease are very striking. These changes were partly due to the ageing of the population which followed as a consequence of falling birth and death rates. The infectious diseases had exacted their principal toll among the young; their gradual disappearance permitted a more general survival into the ages when degenerative and neoplastic diseases occur. Nevertheless, the changes cannot be explained wholly or even mainly in terms of a changing age composition of the population. At all ages there has been a decline in the mortality from infectious diseases and a rise in that from several of the important degenerative and neoplastic diseases. The patterns of mortality have shown changes which argue profound changes in the patterns of causation of fatal diseases.

Some comment is required concerning the virtual restriction of this discussion to statistics of the causes of death. As we saw in an earlier chapter, statistics of mortality were among the first indices of national health to be available on any substantial or reliable scale. Statistics of non-fatal diseases were, for a long time, confined to those diseases that were compulsorily notifiable as infectious or industrial diseases. We have no reliable, comprehensive data on the occurrence of non-fatal disease until quite recent times. This is less important in a historical context than it would be if we sought to establish contemporary patterns of disease variation, because the important diseases of a century ago were liable to be fatal and data on the causes of death are probably useful indicators of the general morbidity. Mortality from the infectious diseases has changed, not so much because of changes in their treatment, but because they now occur far less commonly than they did.

Any more detailed consideration of the changes in diagnoses associated with mortality would have the disadvantage that the diagnostic terms may not be adequately comparable. Fortunately, interpretation of the major trends in mortality may be based on changes in its age and sex distribution. It is unlikely that the recording of age and sex has been so inconsistent as to invalidate their study.

Sex differences in mortality have been available for study since the earliest mortality data was published. No doubt the distinction was originally made because a number of causes of death are limited or partly limited to one sex. The differences have continued to be interesting, particularly in respect of those diseases which are not sex limited but which show different levels of occurrence in the two sexes or a different history. From the historical point of view, sex differences have the virtue that there is little reason to doubt the consistent recording of sex with the passage of time. Available data show increasing differences between sex specific death rates both crude and age specific. In Britain, whereas female rates for all causes together have been steadily falling for the past one hundred years, the rates for males ceased to fall some twenty years ago and have since shown a slight tendency to rise. There seems little doubt that the differences are mainly due to sex specific differences in morbidity from coronary artery disease and lung cancer. But the consequences of these trends may be more important than their causes. They result in a continuing change in the age and sex structure of the population so that there is an increasing preponderance of females among the elderly. By the end of the present century we may expect females to outnumber males in the ratio 2:1 at ages over sixty-five years. The social implications of an elderly population consisting so disproportionately of females, have been relatively little considered. They will include not only the difficulty of ensuring personal economic independence but also the problems arising from social isolation of people in whom a high rate of progressive disability may be expected. As we shall see later, the problems of progressive illness among the elderly are already urgent.

Changes in the association of mortality with age have been particularly striking over the past one hundred years. There has been a drastic reduction in mortality between the ages of one month and about fifty years. Those who survive the neo-natal period are now relatively unlikely to die before late middle age, whereas a hundred years ago, mortality was much more evenly distributed throughout the age range and remained relatively high during adolescence and early adult life. This remarkable change has been examined by McKeown[14] who concluded that it has been the consequence of a substantial reduction in the contribution of environmentally determined morbidity in post-natal life. Genetically determined diseases are less likely to be important as causes of mortality occurring before the end of the reproductive life because fatal inherited illnesses at this period of life would become rare because they would reduce the opportunity of their exhibitors to transmit their causes to the next generation. By the same token, the relatively small effect that environmental changes have had on the mortality of later life may be due to the much larger contribution of genetically determined causes at these ages. Genetically determined diseases could have become common if they were confined to later life, since mortality associated with them would occur after the opportunity had been taken to transmit the causal processes to the next generation. If the genetic component in the causation of diseases of the elderly is large, we may have to accept that many important diseases of the present and immediate future are not amenable to direct preventive action and that control of community health may in future depend to a much greater extent on the treatment of disease and on how we succeed in making it generally available.

But part of the reason that the diseases of later life have shown little response to environmental amelioration may well be that we have not yet succeeded in altering those features of the environment that are relevant. In particular, it seems possible that the causes of much of the important fatal morbidity of adult life today may lie in environments which we personally select for ourselves. If genetically determined susceptibility to particular diseases is complicated by precipitating causes lying in personal behaviour, then it is not surprising that much of the morbidity we suffer today has so far proved difficult to prevent. It is easy to see that the kind of social action taken by the pioneers of nineteenth-century public health against disease agents in the external environment, is difficult to organize against present day diseases. The crucial difference is that the features of the environment that had to be changed in the last century had for long been accounted undesirable on aesthetic grounds, before it was at all clearly understood that they might exert an adverse influence on health. Thus, there existed a social consensus in favour of the necessary social action and the filth of cities and the contamination of water supplies could be tackled with every hope of public support. The behavioural factors that are important in morbidity today, often involve widely enjoyed pleasures such as smoking, over-eating and under-exercise, whose desirability may be thought of as outweighing any risk they represent. Even in the very long run, it is unlikely that humanity will develop a genetically determined repugnance for these pleasures, as to some extent it may have done for human filth, since these habits predominantly influence mortality in the post-reproductive period of life, whereas human filth mainly affected mortality in earlier life when the selective effect would be maximal.

There is an additional consideration that at first seems discouraging. It is quite clear that the environmental factors

involved in many of the important diseases of the present day
are very widely prevalent and that an unfavourable consequence of exposure to them has a low overall probability. As
an example, we may take lung cancer. It is almost certain
that the majority of cases of the disease are substantially due
to cigarette smoking but at the same time, the proportion of
smokers who contract the disease is very small. Since the
habit is pleasant and widespread and the risk of lung cancer
is relatively small, it is extremely difficult to justify the indis-
criminate discouragement of cigarette smoking and, for similar
reasons, it is difficult to accomplish. Since the social pressures
that reinforce the adoption of cigarette smoking are easier to
exploit in the promotion of the habit than they are to counter-
act, it seems a forlorn hope that the disease may ever be preventable. But there is a hope nevertheless. If individuals exist
who may be at especially high risk of the disease it might be
possible to direct preventive action specifically at them. As we
shall see later, there is evidence that the risk of cancer associated with smoking may vary between individuals and there
is hope of eventually being able to identify those at high risk.
The implication of this is that preventive techniques may
eventually be directable at specifically selected individuals
who may be at risk. This raises new possibilities for preventive
medical practice since there may well be other important
diseases which arise from the exposure of specifically susceptible individuals to a particular environmental hazard.

Similar implications are also raised by the question of mortality in very early life. As we have seen, this has remained
relatively unaffected by environmental change. Because of the
effects of genetic selection it is unlikely that genetic causes are
particularly important in determining fatal morbidity at this
period of life, and it is likely therefore that mortality is substantially determined by the circumstances of prenatal and
intranatal experience. Indeed, as we shall see later, there is
good evidence of the importance of environmental causes in
determining the principal causes of death at this period.
These causes include congenital malformations, prematurity,
asphyxia and birth injury, which are conditions that are either

evidently environmental or have been shown to be associated with such indices of environmental causation as season, social class and birth order within the family.

Social class is a particularly important correlate of perinatal mortality.[15] Despite progressive improvements in perinatal mortality over the past twenty five years, the differences between the classes have remained unaffected. For many causes of perinatal death, infants whose parents are from class V have from twice to five times the risk of dying in the perinatal period as infants whose parents are from class I. The importance of this difference is difficult to exaggerate; for example, if all births in Scotland were subject to the perinatal death rates enjoyed by class I births, there would be about 1,500 fewer deaths each year. This would represent a much greater saving of lives than could be achieved by the eradication of congenital malformations; it represents some three times the total annual number of deaths in road accidents, and would represent a total saving of years of human life comparable with that which would be achieved by the abolition of all deaths from cancer. Because a large part of this excess mortality derives from causes which are preventable by good obstetric care during pregnancy and delivery, it must be concluded that the prevention of such mortality depends on identifying and altering the factors that determine the effective availability of good care. There seems little doubt that among these factors are the educational, psychological and social background of the mother and the attitude of doctors to their role in a national health service.

In considering morbidity that is not fatal we are handicapped by the relative recentness of available objective data and by the fact that much the greater part of our data on morbidity relates to the use of medical care rather than to the occurrence of sickness. The bias thus inherent in much of our data is quite important, since self-selection for presentation to the health services still constitutes a largely unknown element in the interpretation of morbidity statisics. This is particularly important at the present time because it is likely that a very large part of all morbidity relates to mental illness and to illness in the elderly, areas in which it is reasonable to suppose that self-selection plays a particularly important part.

Some evidence of the importance of this consideration so far as concerns mental illness may be obtained from consideration of mental hospital admission rates during the past half century. The increase from 80 per 100,000 in Scotland in 1901 to 280 per 100,000 in 1961 cannot conceivably be attributed to a commensurate increase in the frequency of serious mental illness. Indeed the incidence of several important mental illnesses must have declined. The rise must be largely due to a changed view of the function of psychiatric care prevalent not only among patients but also among their doctors. Changes over a more recent period are even more difficult to interpret since a progressive tendency to shorter durations of hospitalization has been accompanied by a rising admission rate. This might be interpreted in terms of a primary effect of recent therapeutic innovations leading to shorter periods of hospitalization which would permit a higher admission rate. Alternatively, the pressure for admission may have resulted in shorter hospital stay, facilitated rather than caused by therapeutic innovations. In either case, the prevalence of hospitalized mental disease may be seen to depend more on the availability of hospital accommodation than on either the prevalence of mental disease or the efficacy of its treatment. The social implications of these changes in the pattern of psychiatric treatment are bound up with changes in the prevalent attitudes to mental illness.

Another large area of morbidity in Britain concerns diseases prevalent among the elderly. A recent study[16] has revealed not only that there is a high prevalence of disability among the elderly but also that relatively little of this disability is known to their general practitioners. The reasons for the discrepancy are far from clear but there is little doubt that much morbidity goes unchecked because of social isolation and because neither patient nor doctor appreciate the potentially progressive nature of many initially trivial disabilities.

The implications of the current state and discernible trends of morbidity may now be summarized. They are:

(a) that control of community health may now depend relatively more on intervention in the course of disease than on primary prevention;

(b) that preventive medicine can no longer be effectively achieved independently of individual co-operation in the maintenance of personal health;

(c) that the efficacy of medical care depends as much on its accessibility as on its technological efficiency.

It is necessary to discuss these implications briefly since they help to explain some of the current and likely future preoccupations of research in social medicine. Research into the causes of disease will eventually concentrate on behavioural factors and on the relationship between heredity and environment. Of particular interest are the diseases of early life because they are common and because they exemplify complex interactions between biological and social influences in the genesis of disease. The diseases of middle age and later life are of interest for similar reasons. Mental illness, which is common, disabling, and probably largely behavioural in its origins, will clearly remain an important preoccupation. But the causation of disease is only part of the necessary understanding on which the response of society to disease will have to be based. Increasingly we shall need to develop research into the consequences of sickness and into the medical and social institutions with which society will tackle the sickness problems it experiences. In particular, research is urgently required into the operation of the health services and their relation to the profession of medicine and to the way in which continuous medical care is provided for the chronic and episodic diseases which are so characteristic of present day morbidity. Whether chronic disability occurs or persists because of failures in medical organization or because of medical ignorance, the care of patients whose illness leaves them with a continuing or residual disability is an unsatisfactory feature of medicine today.

The difficulties are generally of two kinds; technical difficulties which include mainly the absence of effective therapeutic devices; and management difficulties which embrace mainly the

difficulties of ensuring continuity of care throughout a pro-
tracted episode of illness. The remedy for difficulties of the
first kind can only be advances in medical technology which
we can justifiably expect in the course of time. The remedy
for difficulties of the second kind is more difficult to prescribe.
Such is the range of specialized diagnostic and therapeutic
procedures required today that a patient seems inevitably to
be attended by a number of doctors each of whom assumes
responsibility for a limited aspect of the total care of the
patient. The result is often that the long-term objective, i.e.
the restoration of the patient to a condition as nearly as
possible like that from which disease removed him, becomes
obscured because it is no one's responsibility. Although the
general practitioner could formerly fulfil the role of overall
manager of his patient's treatment, the complexity of modern
medicine is making this role increasingly difficult. The general
practitioner is excluded from much of the care of his patient
not only because of administrative arrangements in the
National Health Service but because it is becoming increasingly difficult for any one doctor to accept a meaningful
responsibility for the wide range of illnesses and treatments
in which his patients may become involved.

The trend towards a more personally directed preventive
medicine similarly involves the personal doctor. It seems
likely that much preventive medicine will involve either the
education of 'at risk' individuals or the earlier detection of
disability arising from progressive disease. These are not
approaches that can be effected by legislation nor by medical
officers remote from the individuals who need to be protected.
But the additional burdens likely to be imposed by these new
responsibilities cannot be lightly accepted without a thorough
re-appraisal of the present divisions between preventive and
therapeutic functions and their arbitrary allocation to doctors
differing in outlook, training and administrative responsibility.
If prevention is tending to become secondary rather than
primary, much of the distinction between preventive and
therapeutic medicine becomes unreal. But most doctors today
are already extended, not so much by the volume as by the

range of their work, and any extension of this range may need to be offset by a narrowing of the field within which it has to be applied.

One of the more important, but neglected, needs in medical thinking and practice today is for an approach to the problems of accessibility of medical care. Many people believed that the creation of a National Health Service abolished the most important barrier between patients and the medical care they require. But it becomes increasingly apparent that appropriate medical care is not always applied where it is needed and that barriers at least as formidable as the fee barrier separate doctor and patient. These barriers are still incompletely understood but they include mutual misunderstanding between patients and doctors as well as the uncertainties of symptomatology and the silent early course of much disease.

Many of these trends point to the need for a closer contact between doctor and patient not so much in the face of technological advance as in support of it. All of the trends point the need for a developed understanding not only of human physiology but of human behaviour. And all of the trends seem to confirm the increasing complexity of modern medicine and the virtual impossibility of an individual acquiring a grasp of more than a small part of it.

Today the doctor inevitably specializes, and inevitably needs to secure for his patients, treatment and other care which he himself cannot provide. It is difficult for doctors to accept this situation gracefully and many resent any imputation that there may be aspects of medicine that they themselves do not understand. But this is perhaps for doctors the most important trend today and it is vital that they should come to terms with it if they are to continue to provide the personal care which is the most important tradition that they have to preserve. But the preservation of such traditions and their integration within the structure of an efficient health service will not be achieved without the most critical appraisal of the problems involved. The task of appraisal is scarcely begun but it is among the most important that confront the research worker in social medicine today.

Chapter 6   Heredity and community health

No account of the causes of the distribution of diseases and of health in human society can be complete unless it embraces the role of heredity. But the mechanisms which determine the transmission of characteristics between generations and which underlie the distribution of these characteristics within communities are complex and still poorly understood. Much of our knowledge of the principles of heredity is derived from studies made on animals which differ fundamentally from man in many important ways, not the least of which is their characteristic social organization and the effect that it has on the mating systems that determine much of the hereditary processes. The influence of environment on the relative capacity of individuals to survive is probably highly particular to each animal species and few species live in a relationship with their environment at all similar to that of man. In man we have the additional complication of conscious intervention in the breeding and survival processes.

The animals on which our general knowledge of heredity chiefly depends have mostly been bred in captivity, are often highly inbred, and have been subject mainly to environmental conditions specifically selected as likely to prove informative. Similarly, the species chosen have been selected for such characteristics as adaptability to laboratory conditions, large family size and short inter-generation intervals. Man has appeared to the geneticist as an unsuitable animal for genetic research since he lacks most of the laboratory animal's virtues, chooses his own mate in a generally uninformative way, and, in many social groups, takes great pains to avoid just the matings which would be genetically most instructive. For these reasons, the study of human heredity has tended to remain the province of medical men and to be pursued very largely in relation to the mode of transmission of the very few diseases that can easily be discerned as occurring in families.

The present work is obviously no place for a complete

account of the principles of human genetics. Nevertheless, it will be useful to consider briefly research into the processes that are relevant to the maintenance of our continued identity as a species, and which determine those features of our variation that are relevant to our experience of disease.

For the present purposes, a greatly simplified account will first be required of the processes of reproduction by which parents pass to their offspring the essential material that determines that they belong to the same species as their parents and display some resemblance to them. Each living human being derives from a single cell which represents the union of two cells derived one from each parent. After union, the new cell grows by successive divisions and by differentiation of the resulting cell lines so that by the time the new organism consists of a very large number of cells these have acquired the various specialized functions that characterize the organs of a living human being. The new individual develops within the uterus of its mother, having elaborated a set of membranous structures in which it is enveloped, and a means of drawing nourishment from the maternal circulation. The latter is accomplished by means of a system of blood vessels which lie in intimate proximity to a matching system developed by the maternal uterus and the two systems together constitute the placenta. By means of the placenta the new individual acquires nutrients and disposes of waste products during his stay in the maternal uterus. He is also necessarily in communication with many of the circulating substances of the maternal blood stream, including hormones, drugs, and certain pathogenic micro-organisms. We may interpret available evidence as suggesting that this maternal environment is crucially important to the development of many features of the new individual.

The parental cells that unite to form a new individual are termed respectively the sperms and ova. Despite their difference in size, the sperm and the ovum are thought to make an approximately equal contribution to the characteristics of the new individual. This contribution is mainly contained in the nuclei of the cells and concentrated into minute structures called chromosomes.

The chromosomes contain the instructions or template from which, by a process of protein synthesis, the new individual will develop. When chromosomes are replicated at successive cell divisions occasional small errors in replication occur. These are called mutations. Most mutations probably result in failure of the resulting cell to develop, but some mutations involve merely a change in transmitted characteristics. Mutations may occur at the cell divisions by which body cells increase in number, or replace cells that have completed their useful lives. If mutations occur in body cells they may result in tumours and it is possible that many tumours arise in this way. If mutations occur in the divisions leading to either sperms or ova and they do not result in cell death, a sperm or ovum containing a mutation may take part in the production of a new individual. By such mechanisms a species may develop new features. If a new feature is advantageous, in that it enhances an individual's chances of survival or reproduction relative to fellow beings who lack the feature, then it is likely to become commoner as successive generations manifest the differential survival. If the new feature is disadvantageous, in that it impairs survival or reproduction, then it will tend to disappear, unless it is maintained within the species by occasional new mutations. The frequency of new mutations is generally low and features that depend on new mutations will be rare. The question of whether a new feature arising in consequence of a mutation is advantageous or disadvantageous depends chiefly on the environment the species inhabits. Thus the variety of which a species may be potentially capable in consequence of genetic mutation is controlled by the environment that it inhabits.

It is possible for a mutation to impair survival without impairing reproduction. This will occur if the effect on survival is not manifest until after the end of the reproductive period. Some mutations may impair survival while enhancing fertility and the persistence of the features deriving from them will present a balance which may be tilted either way by circumstances which affect either fertility or survival. Some mutations may confer advantages in some environments but be disadvantageous in others. In this way, environment may determine the distribution of genetically transmitted characteristics. Skin pigmentation is an example of a genetically transmitted characteristic whose world-wide distribution probably reflects the effect of differences in environment. Dark skin may be an advantage in sunny areas where pale skinned people might suffer skin damage; light skin may be an advantage in sunless areas where dark skinned people might suffer from the nutritional effects of inadequate solar irradiation. The introduction of adequate solar protection in the one case and an adequate diet in the other will eliminate the biological relevance of skin colour.

It is now easy to see why disadvantageous characteristics attributable to simple genetic mutations are usually rare unless their effect is delayed until after the end of reproductive life. Characteristics whose manifestation is so delayed are rarely unaffected by the environment which has been inhabited in earlier life and thus are often not easily recognizable as genetically determined. This explains why simply inherited but serious diseases are rare; why common inherited abnormalities are usually trivial in their effect on survival; and why the contribution of heredity to the common serious diseases is usually complex and inextricably bound up with environmental determinants which further complicate the picture.

It is quite wrong to suppose that we may recognize a disease or other characteristic as genetically determined by its tendency to be concentrated in families. The common cold and tuberculosis show familial concentration as do malnutrition and bronchitis. In each case the explanation of the familial concentration lies mainly in the tendency of human families to share a common environment of which an important part is the family itself. It is also wrong to suppose that defects or diseases that are present at birth are usually genetically determined. At birth, an individual has been exposed for forty weeks to a potentially hostile environment at a time of active development. If the defect is severe and at all common, it is unlikely to be simply genetically determined for the reasons given earlier. We cannot therefore recognize diseases as genetically determined by their occurrence either at birth or among members of the same family. Even simultaneous occurrence in identical twins cannot unreservedly be accepted as evidence that a disease is genetically determined since twins share the same uterus at the same time, and identical twins share a common placenta and often an identical upbringing. The recognition that a disease has a substantial genetic component in its causation is nearly always difficult and often impossible. Much of the difficulty in research into the hereditary basis of human disease and its population distribution lies in the difficulty, first of recognizing the contribution of heredity, then of identifying its extent and finally of unravelling its interaction with environmental factors.

Nevertheless there are a large number of human characteristics which are transmitted from parents to offspring by genetic processes but the distribution of which within a population is largely controlled by the environment which the population has inhabited. The simple effects that may be attributed to single genetic mutations will only be common if they do not influence survival or fertility. In this case they will usually be of little medical interest in normal circumstances. But circumstances may change. For example, the ABO blood groups are transmitted quite simply. They have a barely detectable influence on survival in nature but came to be of medical interest because of the introduction of blood transfusion. Transfusion of blood from persons of incompatible ABO groups is dangerous to the recipient. The discovery of this prompted a search for other similar blood group systems. The most important medical consequence of this search has been the discovery of the rhesus blood groups which do account for a relatively uncommon but frequently fatal disease of the newborn which results from a foetus' red blood cells being destroyed by antibodies in the maternal circulation. Although the rhesus blood groups are simply inherited, the disease to which they can give rise has a complex causation which usually involves that the sufferer is at least the second rhesus positive baby born to a rhesus negative mother and which seems to require certain additional circumstances such as that mother and child are ABO compatible and that red cells ofthe first rhesus positive baby escaped into the maternal circulation. Thus, a set of environmental circumstances complicates the simple correspondence between genetic characteristic and associated disease and has prevented the lethal consequences of being rhesus negative from drastically lowering the frequency of this blood group.

Another simply inherited disease of very great interest is sickle cell anaemia. This is a lethal anaemia which occurs in offsprings who have received the genetic causal factor from both of their parents. It is virtually confined to the inhabitants of tropical Africa and is very common in some areas where malaria is also common. The existence of a common, lethal and apparently simply inherited disease at first seemed difficult to explain since the almost invariable early death of affected individuals should reduce the prevalence of the genetic causal factor to very low levels. The explanation came when it was observed that the areas where the disease was highly prevalent were also areas where malaria was endemic at very high levels. Investigations showed that this correspondence was remarkably close, and it was eventually shown that individuals who inherit the sickle cell factor from only one parent and whose blood shows a trivial abnormality which is only detectable by laboratory tests, enjoy a substantial immunity from malaria. This advantage, which they enjoy over persons who do not inherit the factor at all, has permitted the factor to remain quite common in highly malarial areas despite the lethal effect of the disease associated with inheritance of the factor from both parents. Thus a balance between advantage and disadvantage is tilted one way or the other by the local level of malaria endemicity, resulting in the disorder being common in areas where malaria is common and rare or unknown elsewhere. Control of malaria may be expected to be accompanied by a progessive reduction in the frequency of sickle cell anaemia since it will permit non-carriers of the factor to survive as well as carriers and so reduce the proportion of offspring who receive the factor from both parents.

Rhesus factor disease and sickle cell anaemia well exemplify the principle that manifestation of genetic variety is controlled by environment. They are relatively simple examples which we happen to understand. It seems very likely that there are many examples that we do not understand, either because they are more complex or because we have yet to stumble upon their explanations. So far as genetic variety not directly related to disease is concerned we know that interactions between heredity and environment may frequently be complex and we no longer usually seek to study human genetics principally by analysis of the occurrence of characteristics in families.

Very many of the human characteristics that depend at least partly on heredity and which we wish to study in the context of social medicine are characteristics in respect of which we cannot readily divide mankind into simple groups in which some possess the characteristic and some do not. For example, the graded characteristics discussed earlier—arterial pressure, height, growth rate, intelligence—are attributes of mankind which vary continuously, for which mean values are commonest, and for which disease states are defined in terms of extreme values. There is considerable evidence of the importance of heredity in determining such characteristics but it is not easy to account for its effects in terms of simple genetic mechanisms. The hereditary basis of such characteristics is usually considered to involve several genetic factors which may or may not be transmitted independently and whose aggregate effect determines the value of the characteristic they control. It is convenient to illustrate such a mechanism by reference to a simple hypothetical example. Suppose that we have two independent factors each of which may affect a characteristic such as height and each of which may be either present or absent in the parental cells from which offspring arise. Individuals receive genetic material from both parents and so in respect of each factor they may receive no dose, a single dose or a double dose of the factor. Thus, for two factors, they may receive anything from no dose to four doses. If the factors are equal in their effect and additive, there will thus be five degrees of effect possible. For example, if presence of a factor promoted tallness in the individual and absence promoted shortness then there could be five different heights governed by such a simple system. If each factor is present as often as it is absent in a particular species then the frequency of individuals with the various possible combinations would be as below:

no factors 1/16
1 factor   1/4
2 factors   3/8
3 factors   1/4
4 factors   1/16

It will be seen that the distribution is symmetrical, the mean value being commonest and the extreme values being rarest. If we now extend the example to three factors, the number of different classes increases to seven since an individual may have any number of factors from none to six. The distribution will remain symmetrical and the mean value will remain commonest while the extreme values will be rarest. If the example is further modified by increasing the number of factors, by introducing inequality in their effects, by modifying their additiveness and by allowing other external influences to modify the characteristic involved, we may readily see how a continuously graded characteristic may have as its hereditary basis a multifactorial mechanism of this general kind.

One of the interests of mechanisms of this kind is that they are less influenced by lethal selection. Even if individuals exhibiting the extreme combination of factors are eliminated in every generation, interbreeding of survivors will ensure that extreme values will occur in the next generation. We have no direct evidence for the existence of such mechanisms in man but the evidence that the model is a good one is very persuasive. Many graded characteristics in human and other populations are distributed in a way which would be consistent with such a model and predictions based on it give good results.

Much the most interesting human graded characteristic that is convenient to measure is intelligence. This attribute is usually measured by submitting individuals to tests and calculating from the results a quantity called the Intelligence Quotient or I.Q. This quantity has been so designed that the mean I.Q. for the individuals of a normal population is 100 and individual I.Q.s will be distributed around the mean in a manner corresponding to a mathematical expression known as the Normal distribution. This distribution is commonly found in nature and many variable quantities are distributed in exactly or approximately this form. The convenience of this fact is that the properties of such a curve are easily expressed in terms of its mean value and an index of scatter around the mean known as the standard deviation. In the case of the I.Q. the standard deviation is usually about 15, from which it can be calculated that approximately 95 per cent of all persons have I.Q.s between 70 and 130. I.Q.s below 70 are considered to be below the normal just as I.Q.s above 130 are considered to be above the normal.

As soon as it was possible to measure intelligence, many workers set out to explore the question of its inheritance. In 1914 Jaederholm and Pearson[17] published results of I.Q. tests on a normal population and on a series of mentally subnormal individuals. The latter were grouped into those in help classes who were high grade defectives and into a lower group of children who were separately looked after. Distributions of I.Q. in the population approximated to the Normal distribution and it was found that the distribution of the I.Q.s of help class children fitted reasonably well into the lower end of this distribution. Actually, about one third of the help class children did not fit well into the normal curve but this was thought to be due to sampling errors. The group with lower intelligence did not fit into the Normal curve. The authors considered that this suggested that low grade intelligence resulted from gross pathological changes whereas the higher grade children represented simply the lower end of the normal distribution of intelligence. They suggested the possibility that the one third of help class children that did not fit the normal distribution might also be due to pathological causes. Similar conclusions were reached in similar work by Lewis[18] in 1933.

This work was followed by several attempts to classify the pathological group by reference to other factors present. Most such efforts gave equivocal results. In more recent years the problem has been explored differently by applications of ideas resulting from work on the genetics of continuous variation.

In 1950 Roberts[19] published data on the I.Q. distribution of children in Bath. The distribution fitted the Normal curve well except at the very lowest ranges where there was an excess of observed children over the numbers predicted by the Normal curve. This was interpreted as showing the superimposition upon a Normally distributed range of intelligence of a group of I.Q.s which may have arisen from influences other than the normal population distribution of intelligence. In addition to these data, Roberts published the results of I.Q. testing of the brothers and sisters of mentally subnormal children. In the case of the severely defective children their I.Q.s averaged 100. In the case of less severely affected children whose own average I.Q. was 77·4 their brothers and sisters had an average I.Q. of 88·1. This is exactly the kind of result we should expect if high grade mental subnormality represented the lower end of a genetically determined Normal distribution of population intelligence while severe subnormality had some essentially accidental cause. This is because brothers and sisters have half their genetic constitution in common and therefore their mean value for a genetically determined graded characteristic should lie half way between that for the population and that for the group whose brothers and sisters are being studied.

Important reservations need to be made before accepting this explanation. The most important is that there is a marked tendency among human beings to select a mate of similar intelligence to their own and this will increase the tendency for I.Q.s of brothers and sisters to resemble each other if genetic or other familial factors play a part in the determination of intelligence.

There is other evidence that intelligence is not wholly inherited. For example, practice in intellectual activity can markedly affect performance in I.Q. tests[20]. Adults who continue full time education into adult life improve their scores relative to their fellows who finish full time education at the age of fifteen. Intelligence is better maintained into old age by people whose occupations are intellectual rather than manual. In all societies, intelligence is associated with social class. So far as adults are concerned this means no more than that class has been defined in terms which reflect intellectual capability or performance. In the case of children, intelligence is to some extent associated with the social class of the parents. This is undoubtedly to a large extent due to the effect of cultural environment on performance in intelligence tests and to the effect of family background on the possibility of exploiting educational opportunity. This is strongly suggested by the fact that I.Q.s of children from the lower social classes often improve as they grow older. Nevertheless, it seems likely that there are correlations between parental and child intelligence which are attributable to genetic causes.

This raises a number of socially interesting questions. It has often been remarked that fertility is inversely correlated with intelligence and that if intelligence is substantially genetically determined this may lead to an intellectual deterioration of the human species. Anxiety on this score is scarcely justified, however, since any genetic basis for intelligence is likely to be multifactorial and therefore much less influenced by such selective pressures. It is also pertinent to note that since we do not yet provide the educational or other facilities which permit us to exploit available intellectual ability, it is premature to be concerned with its possible decline.

Hypertension affords an example of the difficulty of research into the hereditary basis of human disease. The observation has been made many times that the disease associated with an unduly high arterial pressure shows a tendency to 'run in families'. Early attempts to elucidate possible patterns of genetic transmission of the disease generally began by assuming that there were no problems in distinguishing patients with hypertension from persons without the disease. For the sake of diagnostic convenience it has been common to adopt an arbitrarily chosen level of arterial pressure above which a patient's pressure is regarded as significantly raised. In the absence of any evident cause for a raised arterial pressure, a person whose pressure exceeded the arbitrary level was described as suffering from essential hypertension. An early enquiry[21] sought to ascertain the frequency of the condition among the first degree relatives of a series of hypertensive patients seen in hospital practice. The frequency of living relatives with hypertension plus those dead relatives whose cause of death seemed likely to have been associated with a raised arterial pressure, approximately to 50 per cent. This would be the expected frequency if the condition were simply determined by dominant, single-factor inheritance. The author of this study concluded that such was probably the cause. More recently it has been pointed out by Pickering[22] and his colleagues that choice of a suitable level for distinguishing normal pressure from abnormal will give any desired proportion of affected relatives. It is therefore important to establish an objectively valid criterion for the distinction. They found it impossible to establish such a criterion in terms of arterial pressure since this was distributed continuously and approximately Normally in a sample drawn from the general population. Moreover, pressure distributions differed continuously as successively older groups of individuals were examined. They interpreted these data as suggesting that arterial pressure is multifactorially determined and that in normal individuals it increases with advancing age. An alternative explanation, advanced by Platt,[23] is that abnormal arterial pressure levels become more frequent as age advances but that the determinants of abnormal pressure are not multifactorial but much simpler. The limiting of their manifestation until later ages is just what one would expect of a fairly lethal, simply inherited but common abnormality. He pointed out that a substantial proportion of the middle aged relatives of middle aged patients with hypertension, themselves have hypertension. Obervations suggesting that arterial pressure in such relatives is bimodally distributed have now largely been discounted as artefacts arising from sampling error and from unconscious errors in measurement, and it is of interest that the pressure distributions of relatives in Platt's data, although bimodal, do not resemble the pressures one would expect in a population composed equally of 'normal' individuals plus individuals with 'hypertension'. Of the two modes, one occurs at the normal level and one occurs half way between the normal level and that in the hypertensive patients. This latter mode is where we should expect it to be if pressure is multifactorially inherited and if essential hypertension is simply the upper end of a Normal distribution of population arterial pressure. The problem is greatly complicated by the fact that essential hypertension may only be defined negatively as raised arterial pressure without evident cause, for the extent to which causes are evident is dependent on the diligence and curiosity of the enquirer. Therefore, any group of people with raised arterial pressures may represent patients with more than one disease. It seems likely that there are simple causes of hypertension which we still cannot isolate, but that a large proportion of patients with raised arterial pressures represent the upper end of a Normally distributed population distribution of pressures.

The issue is further complicated by the undoubted importance of environmental determinants of the level of arterial pressure. Pressure is higher in those who drink alchohol than in those who do not and lower in those who smoke cigarettes than in those who do not.[24] It is also higher in people of above average body weight. A finding of great interest but which poses considerable difficulties of interpretation is that pressures are lower for people who have had children than for those who have not and that this is more marked for fathers than for mothers. Pressures measured at five year intervals show a smaller rise for persons who have become parents in the interval than for those who have not.

The importance of distinguishing between multi-factorial and simpler causes of disease lies principally in the contribution which such a distinction may make to the problem of deciding whether future research might be better directed towards establishing a cause and a possible primary preventive technique or towards developing techniques for earlier diagnosis and better treatment. Generally speaking, simply caused diseases are more likely to prove preventable while multifactorially determined diseases are better tackled by earlier diagnosis and more effective treatment. This is the case whether the causation is largely environmental or largely hereditary.

It seems generally likely that the factors that are involved in single factor and in multifactorial inheritance are similar and that they consist of particular configurations of molecules in the structure of the chromosomes. Since we are still very far from being able to carry out useful studies of the relationship between these molecules and their effects on individuals and populations, it is usual to think of the chromosomes as carrying entities that are called genes. Mutants are therefore thought of as genes whose effects have been changed. As we have seen, the persistence of a gene in a changed form will depend on whether its effects are advantageous or disadvantageous in the prevailing environment. It will also depend on whether it exerts its characteristic effect on individuals who have received it from only one of their parents or whether it needs to have been received from both parents before its effect is manifest.

The distribution of genes in a population depends on the history of the species, on its genetic mutations, on the effect of environment in determining the advantages and disadvantages of the various genetic features which have arisen and on factors which may have fostered or limited particular mating patterns. We know relatively little about genetic mutation except that we have been able to estimate the frequency with which some genes mutate and we know from animal experiments that a number of environmental influences (e.g. ionising radiations) may influence the frequency of mutations. Since we are still far from clear which features of our variation are largely genetically transmitted we still do not know very clearly how the environment limits this variation. Until comparatively recently we knew very little about mating preferences and restrictions and even less about their genetic effects. The study of the genetic structure of human populations has therefore been confined largely to the comparison of observed distributions of characteristics with those expected from very simple theoretical assumptions. The characteristics have usually been chosen for their convenience in study rather than for their interest as determinants of important issues in the survival of the human species. Since many of the characteristics that have been studied have been of trivial importance in respect of survival, their distribution has usually been found to conform with that expected from the simple assumptions that have been made. These have usually been that the distribution of genes follows a random pattern comparable to that which would be expected if each new individual acquired his genetic make up by drawing genes at random from a pool of those constituting the parent generation's genetic make up. Departures from this basic pattern in the case of particular genes are usually interpreted as implying either that the gene is undergoing a change in its frequency or that mating is not random with respect to it. Changes in gene frequency imply either a change in the mutation rate or a change in the balance of advantage and disadvantage associated with the gene. Such changes in balance occur as a result of environmental change; the change in the frequency of sickle cell gene that we may expect as a result of malaria control is an example. Departures from random mating are rarely identified by genetic enquiry and are more usually postulated on sociological grounds.

In the absence of changes of the kinds discussed in the previous paragraph, the genetic structure of populations should remain constant. This was first formulated as a law and proved by the two workers, Hardy and Weinberg. Their discoveries were made independently but virtually simultaneously and the law bears the joint name of the Hardy Weinberg law. Its utility in human population genetics has principally been conceptual; it is not usually possible to detect the departures from it that would indicate the presence of factors which promote genetic change. Variations in the distribution of genes among the inhabitants of different people of the earth indicate past influences which have modified population genetic structure and some of these may be guessed at fairly plausibly. The charting of population genetic structure may become much more important in the future.

Among the more important influences which may affect population genetic structure in the foreseeable future are changes in mating patterns which may follow improvements in human communication. These improvements relate to increased opportunities for travel and migration, as well as to changes in socially determined attitudes to mating choice. The most important genetically determined variation among the human species at the present time relates to skin colour but the significance of this variation is social and political rather than biological. Technical changes which may reduce the relevance of skin colour to climate and habitat may be expected to augment social changes in altering the distribution of the relevant genes over future generations.

Perhaps the most important influence on population genetic structure will be the practice of medicine. Preventive and curative medicine both aim at changing the environment so as to affect survival. This cannot but alter the relative advantages and disadvantages associated with particular genes. We have already discussed the example of sickle cell anaemia. There are doubtless others. For example, the introduction of insulin treatment in the treatment of diabetes must affect the survival of patients with this disease and permit the freer transmission of any associated genes. Efforts to improve infant mortality and stillbirth rates are likely to increase the frequency of any genes that are associated with such early death. It has often pessimistically been argued, that for this reason, all effort devoted to medical advance is self-defeating, since we may succeed merely in perpetuating undesirable genes. But this is a fallacy which arises from the unjustifiable notion that there are bad genes and good genes. Genes are only bad or good in relation to the environment in which they are manifested. If the environment is favourable to them they will survive and if it is unfavourable they will not. If we have made the environment favourable to particular genes then they are no longer to be considered bad genes. And if we have not, then they will not become more common. Medical treatment and preventive medicine operate by changing the environment. An environment which includes insulin is more favourable to the survival of the genes associated with diabetes than an environment in which it is lacking. We cannot really influence the frequency of a gene except by improving the survival and fertility of its exhibitors. If this means that more people live long enough to have children it is difficult to see that this is in any sense a self-defeating achievement.

It is also worth noting that in the case of sickle cell anaemia we might have viewed the process differently had we discovered the effect of the gene in protecting against malaria before we discovered its effect in causing anaemia. Had it been known that there was a gene conferring a substantial protection against malaria, and that it was particularly common in areas of high malarial endemicity, there would doubtless have been those who could have argued against malaria control on the grounds that it would lead to genetic deterioration of the species. That malaria control will also lower the frequency of sickle cell anaemia is an interesting confirmation of a view expressed by Haldane, that loss to the species of genes that are no longer required may permit the acquisition of new genes which may confer benefits.

Perhaps the most interesting implication of the relation between genes and the environment in which they are expressed is in the field of preventive medicine. Experience suggests that it is very much easier to change our environment than our genes. The control of diseases with a genetic basis may well have to depend on our altering the environment in which the effects of genes are manifested. So far as medical treatment is concerned, this simply means applying available treatments for diseases and is in no way dependent on our even knowing that specific genes are involved. In the case of preventive medicine we are beginning to face the difficult problems of those diseases of later life whose causation seems likely to be at least partly genetic since they have remained after environmental change has greatly reduced morbidity in the pre-reproductive period of life. These diseases are often crucially determined by specific environments which may exert their effects only on susceptible individuals. Avoidance of the specific environmental agencies that are dangerous may be possible only for a few individuals who can be identified as at risk. For example, it seems likely that lung cancer arises when susceptible individuals are exposed to cigarette smoking. It is impracticable to eliminate cigarette smoking from everyone's environment and might be unjustifiable if only a small proportion of individuals are at risk. Identification of such susceptible individuals would permit them to avoid smoking, and anti-smoking advice might well be effective if its specific relevance to individuals could be guaranteed. What we presently lack is a means of identifying susceptible individuals, but it is not impossible that we shall develop such techniques.

Unfortunately, exploration of the genetic contribution to human variability is beset with difficulty and progress is slow. Examples given later of findings that bear on the question will show, however, that progress is being made.

Chapter 7   The environment before birth

Study of the influence of the post-natal environment has produced the major triumphs of public health over the past one
hundred years. But human life does not begin at birth. At
birth, man is already a complex creature whose functioning
and development have been subjected to a variety of influences
for some forty weeks. Among these influences there are many
with a direct bearing on the development of pathological conditions; there are many that influence normal growth and development. Differences in the degree of maturity at birth and
the occurrence of developmental malformations in the newborn
provide evidence of the extent to which the prenatal environment may vary; the study of these environmental variations
has recently been engaging much attention.

The problem is important. With the reduction in child
mortality that has taken place during recent years, a reduction that has largely proceeded from our better understanding
of the influence of the post-natal environment, it is becoming
increasingly clear that continuation of the decrease will in
future depend on an increased understanding of factors that
operate before and during birth itself. The proportion of
foetuses alive at the twenty-eighth week of gestation that are
lost before the age of one year is of the order of 5 per cent. A
further 3 per cent are malformed at birth but survive into post-
natal life. We do not know exactly, but the proportion of all
conceived individuals that are lost in early pregnancy is almost
certainly even higher. Loss from abortion is generally estimated at around 15 per cent of all conceptions. At the present
time we view this earlier loss of human life remarkably philosophically, as child mortality is often viewed in societies where
it seems inescapably high. But it represents a wastage of
human life nevertheless. It is reasonable to suppose that a
large part of this wastage would be preventable by environmental control if we understood better the environmental influences that are relevant.

The study of the prenatal environment in man is therefore an area of enquiry that is of particular interest and concern. Unfortunately, it presents a number of difficulties. A major difficulty is the general impossibility of systematic direct observation. Direct observation has always been accidental and of brief duration, and has consisted for the most part of studies made of aborted foetuses and occasionally of pregnant uteri that have been removed surgically. Although our knowledge of human embryology has been very dependent on such opportunities for observation there are a number of obvious limitations that are imposed by the abnormal situations that such opportunities imply.

Radiographical, biochemical and, more recently, electronic and acoustic methods have also been employed. But such techniques have a limited application to the problems that are most relevant to the study of foetal development. Studies of laboratory animals have also been fruitful but their relevance must always remain in serious doubt since few of the animals that are readily available for research resemble man in such important respects as duration of gestation and degree of maturity at birth.

For these reasons and for others, the study of the influence of the prenatal environment in man has owed a great deal to epidemiological enquiries. Availability of simple data on the circumstances of pregnancy and delivery has been an important reason for this. The prenatal environment is essentially the maternal uterus and circulation and these are themselves influenced by the environment inhabited by the mother. Care of the pregnant woman has been a feature of medical activity in nearly all societies of which we are aware and for as long as historical evidence has been available. The health of the mother and her experience during pregnancy are now known to have a considerable influence on the development of her child.

From the literature that has now accumulated from social medical enquiry into the effects of the prenatal environment, it is not possible in the present work to do more than select examples. These will be taken from three fields which have been particularly productive and which exemplify many of the features of such research. They are: the determinants of the maturity of foetuses at birth; the environmental circumstances associated with anencephaly and the influence of X-ray exposure before birth on the development of malignant disease in childhood.

Maturity at birth

Among the important causes of perinatal death and of a substantial amount of morbidity in post-natal life is the phenomenon of 'premature' birth. 'Prematurity' is usually defined in terms of birth weight and among people of European origin the definition commonly adopted is that a weight of 5½ pounds (2,500 grm.) or less, denotes prematurity. This criterion, which was suggested as long ago as 1920 by Ylppö,[25] has been accepted ever since, chiefly because it is relatively easy to determine birth weight with reasonable accuracy. Acceptance has generally been justified by the observation that although about one third of all babies whose birth weight is below 5½ pounds are born after a normal period of gestation, their survival beyond birth is substantially poorer than that of babies of greater weight.

A great deal of what we know about the normal determinants of birth weight in man is due to the work of McKeown and his colleagues in Birmingham. Their work, which was published over a period of some ten years, is largely based on observations recorded in respect of births in that city. Data were obtained from a number of sources and these differed for different parts of the work. They will be discussed in the following paragraphs as the conclusions based upon them are described.

In 1947 an attempt was made to record for all births to mothers resident in Birmingham, details of place of birth, sex of child, whether live or stillborn, whether multiple or single birth, the date of the last menstrual period of the mother, her age and the number of her previous births, the weight of the child at birth and other simple observations. These data were obtained in respect of most of the rather more than 23,000 births in the city for that year.

A number of important findings emerged from analysis of these data.[26] When births are distributed by birth weight and duration of gestation the correlation between the two is high. The shape of the curve of mean birth weight plotted against duration of gestation is S-shaped. For the earliest recorded stages of gestation, the increase of weight with duration of gestation is relatively slow. After the 29th week there is a steady linear increase in weight until about the 40th week, after which the increase falls off and weight remains nearly constant for each successive week of gestation. It is thus evident that growth becomes relatively restricted in late pregnancy.

The association of birth weight with birth order and with mother's age is marked.[27] The older the mothers the heavier the mean weight of their babies, and the smaller the proportion of babies whose weight is below $5\frac{1}{2}$ pounds. A similar association occurs with increasing birth order. First births are, on average, lightest and the mean birth weight is greater for second and still greater for third or later births. At each birth order, birth weight seems little affected by mother's age but at each maternal age birth weight increases with birth order. This is consistent with what is known to be the case in most other species in which successive offspring born to the same mother are progressively heavier.

There is a difference between the mean birth weights for male and female children; male children weigh on average about a quarter of a pound more than females. The difference cannot be due to a longer duration of gestation since, in fact, this is slightly shorter for male infants. In fact, at all durations of gestation, the mean birth weight was greater for males than for females. There are differences in weight at birth, therefore, between males and females and between first born and later born; neither difference is accounted for by differences in duration of gestation. These weight differences must therefore be dependent on differences in rates of growth.

It is clear that the weight of an individual at birth may be affected by the duration of the associated pregnancy and by the rate of foetal growth. Differences in birth weight from both sources have been demonstrated by the data so far considered.

In addition, an interaction effect has been shown in that rate of increase in weight falls off in late pregnancy. The determinants of weight at birth, and therefore of capacity to survive, must involve a complex interaction between growth rate and duration of pregnancy.

Since it is well known that twins are born at lower mean weights than single babies and after a shorter pregnancy, it is of interest to study the problem in multiple births. McKeown and his colleagues[28] next assembled data on birth weight, duration of gestation and number of foetuses. Since triplets and quadruplets are relatively rare, the data from Birmingham required to be augmented. In addition to data on 17,072 single births and 506 twin births from Birmingham, data on 218 triplet maternities were obtained by enquiry from all hospitals in Britain with more than fifty beds. Data on 24 quadruplet maternities were obtained with the assistance of the national press and by writing to the hospitals where they were born. These data confirmed the well known finding that the mean birth weight of the individual babies is smaller as the number in the uterus increases; the mean weights for single, twin, triplet and quadruplet babies were 7·4 pounds, 5·3 pounds, 4·0 pounds and 3·1 pounds respectively. In this respect, man resembles other species. The durations of gestation are progressively shorter as the number of foetuses increases, so that part of the difference in weight is easy to explain. But the differences in duration of gestation do not explain the whole of the weight differences. From curves fitted to the data it is evident that birth weight is independent of the number of foetuses in the uterus until about the 27th week of pregnancy. Furthermore, the association between birth weight and duration of gestation flattens out earlier for quadruplets than for triplets, earlier for triplets than for twins and earlier for twins than for single births. At the stage at which this flattening out occurs, the total mean weight of the occupants of the uterus is the same whatever their number and is about 7 pounds. This suggests that the growth of the foetuses remains unrestricted whatever their number until their total weight is about 7 pounds. Thereafter, their growth is restricted—presumably by the capacity of the uterus to support it. Maturity at birth, defined in terms of birth weight, is thus determined partly by the foetal capacity to grow but also by the maternal capacity to support that growth and by the duration of the period during which growth occurs.

The mechanism is therefore one in which the crucial limits are set by the uterine environment and by how long it is inhabited by the growing foetus. The mechanism that determines the onset of labour is therefore of great interest.

The data on multiple births are especially interesting. The simplest view we might take of the mechanism of the onset of labour is that the uterus expels its contents when it can no longer support their growth. McKeown's data make it clear that this is not the case. He pointed out that if this were so, then the total birth weight ought always to be about the same however many foetuses are carried. But this is not so. The greater the number of foetuses, the greater is their total weight, despite the progressively shorter durations of gestation for greater numbers of foetuses. Whereas single births have a mean weight at birth of 7·4 pounds after 280 days gestation, quadruplets have a total mean weight of 12·3 pounds after 237 days gestation. McKeown suggested a possible explanation of these findings. This is that the uterus may become progressively more sensitive to the bulk of its contents as pregnancy advances. Thus, the fewer the foetuses, the longer they will remain *in utero;* the larger the number, the shorter their stay. Such a mechanism would be inherently self regulating and might also explain the relative rarity of multiple birth in man, since any genetically determined tendency to multiple birth would suffer from the selective effect of the greater mortality associated with more premature birth.

Later work by McKeown[29] on a large series of single births explored another aspect of the question of foetal growth. Prenatal and post-natal growth rates were compared and it was shown that the foetal growth curve is linear until about the 36th week of pregnancy, after which it falls away. After birth, the growth curve resumes its linear form parallel to the linear curve before 36 weeks. McKeown interpreted this as showing that until 36 weeks the uterus does not restrict inherent growth capacity of the foteus, but that beyond 36 weeks the uterine environment is inadequate to support the full foetal growth capacity. After birth this restriction is removed and the new individual's growth capacity may re-exert its influence.

Naturally, the questions raised by this include that of what agency on the foetus mediates a restricting influence on growth. It is natural to direct first attention to the placenta, via which the nutritional needs of the foetus are transmitted and which is available after birth for such observations as its weight to be recorded. The study of the influence of placental weight on foetal weight was an obvious next step. Observations were made on foetal and placental weight for 4,931 single live births. It was found that birth weight was related to placental weight and both were related to duration of gestation. The relationship between birth weight and placental weight differed between the sexes and between first born and later born. At placental weights below 1 pound there is no difference between male and female birth weights but at higher placental weights there is a steadily increasing difference in that males are heavier than females. McKeown's explanation of this is as follows. When the placenta is very small it is unable to meet the growth needs of either males or females. The larger the placenta, the greater the proportion of foetuses that have their growth needs fully met. Since males are usually heavier than females it must be assumed that the proportion of females whose needs are fully met is greater than that of males at any given placental weight and that therefore the difference in weight between the sexes changes with the changing proportion of foetuses exhibiting their full growth rate. At higher placental weights, where sex differences in birth weight are greatest, it must be assumed that a larger proportion of foetuses of both sexes are exhibiting their full growth capacity. This may be tested. Since we have seen that restriction of growth occurs mainly in the later weeks of pregnancy it would be expected that restrictions would be less at earlier weeks and would be demonstrated by a larger sex difference in earlier than in later weeks. This is so. The sex difference for births at 34 to 37 weeks was 0·4 pounds at constant placental weight and at 38 to 41 weeks only 0·07 pounds.

Males are heavier than females and later born are heavier than first born. The sex difference is presumably of genetic origin and would be expected to be maintained after birth; the birth order difference is presumably related to the intra-uterine environment and should diminish after birth or at least not increase. McKeown and his colleagues have shown that both these expectations are confirmed by available data.

We have now sufficient evidence of the operation of both genetic and environmental factors in determinating birth weight, and some understanding of their respective contributions. What further can we state about the intra-uterine environmental circumstances in terms of observations made on mothers? In 1938, Walton and Hammond[30] described the results of reciprocal crosses between Shire horses and Shetland ponies obtained by artificial insemination. Birth weight and duration of gestation of offspring followed the pattern of the maternal animal. This suggests that at least in these animals the maternal intra-uterine environment is the more important factor determining maturity at birth and its influence must be understood and accounted for before we can examine the genetic contribution. Is the same true of man? We can test this by examination of correlations between birth weight and the size of the two parents. McKeown and his colleagues[31] have shown that for man, correlations between paternal and foetal size are minimal at birth and increase during post-natal life. Correlations between maternal and foetal size are maximal at birth, being much larger than those between paternal and foetal size, and they decrease during post-natal life. These results suggest that at birth, the equilinearity expected if birth weight were purely genetic, is modified because the mother provides not only genes but also environment. Equilinearity is restored later in life when the environment ceases to be largely a function of maternal characteristics.

The series of investigations reported by McKeown and his colleagues, together with reports by other workers using similar data and techniques, have permitted a remarkably complete account to be given of the processes which determine the maturity of newborn individuals in a normal population. There can be little doubt that a substantial proportion of 'prematurity' represents the lower extreme of the population distribution of birth weight together with the effect of multiple birth. Nevertheless, we now require to know more of the possible contribution of abnormal or remediable influences which may determine especially low birth weight. For example, the influence of the mother's social and physical environment, her nutrition and her health during pregnancy are still far from clear although such influences are undoubtedly important. Research in this and in related fields continues.

Environmental influences in anencephaly

Study of the aetiology of human congenital malformations has largely been pursued by the methods of social medicine. Among these malformations the commonest, and one of the most lethal, is anencephaly, in which there is a major failure of development of the anterior part of the central nervous system and which is incompatible with post-natal survival for more than a few hours. The majority of cases result in still-birth and account for some 12 to 15 per cent of all stillbirths. The occurrence of this malformation is particularly distressing for the parents who may frequently, in consequence, be reluctant to embark upon another pregnancy. The obstetrician's responsibility to advise the parents on the desirability of such a course is often complicated by uncertainty about the risks involved and by lack of a clear comprehension of the relative influence of environmental and genetic factors in the genesis of the condition.

A very large proportion of all the studies that have been carried out to investigate this condition have been based on data from the certification of the causes of stillbirth in Scotland where certification of these causes began in 1939. The condition is easy to diagnose and uniformly fatal so that the available data are likely to be reliable and representative. Tabulations of data on causes of stillbirth in relation to maternal age, birth order, season, region, social class and other variables have been published in the Annual Reports of the Registrar General for Scotland and special tabulations have also been prepared for research workers. A number of authors have made use of these data, notably R. G. Record[32] and J. H. Edwards,[33] and the former has also published studies deriving from data from other sources. Important contributions have also been made by MacMahon[34] using data from Rhode Island, U.S.A., and by Coffey[35] from Dublin.

The first point to emerge from study of annual data is the variation in incidence from year to year. For example, the incidence has been higher in recent years than formerly. The rates were, in fact, at their lowest in the period 1940 to 1950 and have been high in the period since 1950. Although a somewhat similar condition can be induced in experimental animals by several dietary deficiencies, there nevertheless seems no evidence that the condition in man is associated with nutritional intake.

Another important association of incidence with time is the marked fluctuation with season. This was first demonstrated by Record and his colleagues[36] in data from both Birmingham and Scotland. The condition is generally much commoner among autumn and winter births than among births in spring and summer. Seasonal variations of this kind may be demonstrated simply by comparing the distribution by month of occurrence with that for all births in the related population.

In the case of anencephaly the season that is of interest is that of the malformation's origin rather than that of birth. It seems certain that the effect upon the developing embryo is exerted at an embryonic age of about three weeks but this may not be the time at which the influence affects the mother. For example, if the cause were a virus condition of the mother which resulted in damage to embryos attaining the age of three weeks at some time after the initial maternal infection then the effective time of action on the mother might be before the child's conception. Nevertheless, it is useful to examine the seasonal fluctuation of the occurrence of the malformation among three week embryos. A difficulty is that the duration of gestation is shorter than for normal births and somewhat variable. Since it has been observed that the sex ratio in anencephaly varies with duration of gestation there may be different causes which operate differentially upon the sexes and determine different durations of gestation. However, if these sources of difficulty are ignored, it seems that three week embryos are particularly affected from March to July and least affected between September and December.

However, the seasonal variation has been subject to occasional changes. For example, in the summer of 1958 the stillbirth rate in Scotland for anencephaly was unusually high. Since this followed by about eight months the epidemic of Asian influenza in the autumn and winter of 1957, speculation was aroused concerning a possible causal relationship. However, the summer incidence remained high in several subsequent years when there had been no autumn epidemic of influenza. Record[32] has examined the possible importance of influenza. He points out that if we take into account the duration of the influenzal illness and of the period during which the embryo is at a stage at which the defect may occur, the duration of the period of risk to an embryo from maternal influenza cannot be less than three or four days. In Scotland, therefore, which has about 100,000 births per year, at least 1,000 embryos would be at risk at any time. The attack rates for influenza among women of reproductive age in the two months October and November, 1957, would involve that about 500 of the births in the following May and June had been suitably exposed to maternal influenza. The excess of cases of anencephaly relative to the mean of the preceding and succeeding years, which were not preceded by autumn influenza, was only 17. Influenza is unlikely, therefore, to be a major cause of anencephaly.

In general, the explanation of seasonal variations in disease occurrence or in other phenomena, often proves difficult. There is a well recognized seasonal variation in the birth rate in Britain in that relatively more births occur in the spring. Since there is a similar seasonal variation in marriages, which arises to some extent because of advantages with respect to income tax relief, it is tempting to conclude that the seasonal variation in the birth rate merely reflects the seasonal variation in marriages and allows approximately one year for marriages to produce a first birth. If this were the cause, one would expect that the seasonal variation would be more marked for first births than for later births. Leck,[37] however, has shown that the amplitude of the seasonal variation increases for successive birth orders. We have very little information on seasonal variation in sexual activity within marriage, but it seems surprising that seasonal variation should be more marked as marriage duration increases.

To return to the problem of anencephaly; the most marked association of incidence is with the social class of the parents. The incidence in social class V is some four times that in social class I. No plausible explanation of this association has been advanced except the possibility that it might arise if the causal agency were an infection.

Other associations of incidence are with maternal age and with birth order. Incidence is high in first pregnancies, lowest in second pregnancies and thereafter rises again so that the highest incidence is recorded for seventh and later pregnancies. A similar picture is seen with respect to maternal age; incidence is high in mothers under 20 years of age, falls to its lowest point among mothers of 25–29 and thereafter rises to reach its highest point at ages 40 and over. Examination of maternal age and birth order separately has shown these associations to be independent of each other.

Analysis of specially prepared tables provided by the Registrar General for Scotland, permitted Record[32] to conclude that all these influences are independent and not determined simply by their mutual association. The demonstration that the disease is thus associated with many different environmental influences permits the clear inference to be drawn that it is substantially environmentally determined.

This is supported by several published records of its occurrence in only one member of a pair of genetically identical twins. But it also raises the difficulty of deciding whether the disease may arise in consequence of a constellation of causal influences or whether it represents several different disease entities each having a different cause. Some additional evidence is provided by the association of anencephaly with spinal bifida which is a similar embryonic defect but of the lower central nervous system. The two diseases occur together frequently in the same individual and there is some evidence that they may occur in the same families; i.e. families in which one disease has occurred may be more likely than average to suffer the other. Nevertheless, spina bifida does not show the same seasonal incidence as anencephaly, is not associated with social class and affects the two sexes much more equally than does anencephaly which is very much commoner in females. An explanation may be that anencephaly associated with spina bifida may have a different cause from anencephaly alone. This would explain other features of the population distribution of the two diseases. For example, the recurrence rate of anencephaly among subsequently born brothers and sisters of an affected individual is about 6 per cent. But among the subsequent brothers and sisters in a family where two cases have already occurred it is much higher. This might be explained if familially concentrated anencephaly were aetiologically distinct.

The assembly of a large series of instances of familial anencephaly is not easy. The circumstances of stillbirth registration and the systems of record storage make it difficult to identify familial cases. Series assembled from local sources rarely permit the identification of enough families to make possible the necessary analyses. The present author has recently assembled the data of the Registrar General for Scotland so that records of still births occurring in the same families are brought together. The record linkage procedure employed is simple once the appropriate family identification data have been recorded, and it may be of interest to describe its main features.[38]

In Scotland, for all registered vital events (births, stillbirths, marriages and deaths) the name, maiden name and mother's maiden name are recorded. Thus two parental names are available in each record. Assembly of records of fraternally related individuals may be begun by assembly of all individuals having the same pair of parental surnames. Individuals whose parents also have the same date of marriage are then likely to be brothers and sisters. Even for a common name such as Smith, which is the commonest name in Scotland, the frequency in the population is somewhat less than 1 in 50. Individuals whose parents are both called Smith will therefore be less frequent than 1 in 2,500, since there is no known tendency for Smiths to marry other Smiths. In Scotland there are about 40,000 marriages a year or an average of 120 per day. Thus, two individuals, each of whose two parents have the same pair of names and date of marriage, are highly unlikely not to be brothers or sisters. For all cases identified as families by this technique it is possible to test additional data for the plausibility of the assumption of relationship. The whole procedure may be programmed to be carried out on electronic computers.

Data assembled in this way for Scottish stillbirths over the period 1948–63 contained records of 125 families with more than one stillbirth due to anencephaly. They have been analysed by season of birth, social class, parental age and birth order as well as by sex. The distributions for the familial cases closely resemble those for cases in general. It is therefore unlikely that familial anencephaly has causes different from those operating where the condition is not familial.

It seems, for the present, that interpretation of the well recognized associations of anencephaly with so many indices of environmental influence must remain difficult. One cannot help feeling that a complete solution of this aetiological puzzle must be very near, but that we still lack either some key piece of information or the imagination necessary to explain the wealth of data that we now possess.

Prenatal X-rays and malignant disease

It has long been recognized, both from animal experiments and from the early experience of workers in radiology, that heavy exposure to X-rays and other forms of ionising radiation may result in the development of malignant tumours. Massive evidence from studies in Hiroshima since the bombing of that city has shown an increase in the incidence of

leukaemia and other malignant diseases. Since, in most societies, the principal source of radiation exposure is from medical
X-rays, it has been of great interest to enquire into the possibility that such exposure may raise the risk of developing
malignant diseases. Evidence that the dose levels used in
X-ray treatment may raise the incidence of leukaemia among
those who receive such treatment was provided by studies by
Court-Brown and his colleagues[39] who found that among
14,000 patients with ankylosing spondylitis that had been
treated by X-rays, 38 cases of leukaemia developed. This is
appreciably more than would occur in a similarly sized sample
from the general population even although the actual risk
involved seems small in relation to the benefit conferred by
the treatment. Nevertheless, the study provides valuable data
for the establishment of the relationship between exposure
dose and its associated effect.

A complete account of this relationship requires the availability of data on the effects of a wide range of X-ray doses.
This is particularly important since we need to know whether
there is a minimum dose below which tumour induction does
not occur. Viewed from the population point of view, quite
small increases in the risk of tumours may be important since
they may appreciably raise the total number of cases. The
importance of diagnostic X-ray is considerable, since although
the usual doses are small, they are very widely given and a
small dose given on a wide scale may produce more additional
tumours in a large population than a much heavier dose given
to fewer people.

In view of the sensitivity of rapidly growing tissues, it
seemed natural to enquire whether diagnostic X-rays reaching
the foetus *in utero* can affect tumour incidence among the
children who develop from such foetuses. Since there are a
number of diagnostic procedures associated with pregnancy
which involve substantial X-ray dosage, the problem is of
practical as well as theoretical importance.

The first important work on this subject was carried out by
Stewart and her colleagues of the Department of Social
Medicine in Oxford University. Their enquiry is worthy of

detailed attention, partly because it illustrates the difficulties of such an enquiry and how they may be tackled and partly because it incurred hostile and often ill-informed criticism. The principal difficulty is that malignant disease in childhood is not a common condition. Any circumstance which was to raise its incidence would therefore be difficult to detect unless the increase were very large. Anticipating this difficulty and accepting the limitations of their available resources, Stewart and her colleagues decided on a retrospective enquiry into the X-ray histories of children who developed malignant disease. Retrospective enquiries make more efficient use of data, especially when the condition under examination is uncommon and the expected variation in its incidence is small. They involve the need for careful consideration of all possible sources of bias in the data that are retrospectively obtained.

Stewart proceeded by attempting to identify all cases of malignant disease leading to death in children age 0–9 years in the years 1953–55 in England and Wales. For this purpose mortality data from the Registrar General are suitable because such diseases are nearly always fatal in children and the deaths of children at this age are invariably carefully scrutinized and therefore reliably certified as to cause. There were 1,694 cases of which 792 were of leukaemia and 902 were of other cancers. For each case, the birth registration entry was located and an adjacently registered child was selected as a control for comparison. Controls were matched for such features as sex, birth order and locality of residence. The parents of cases and controls were then interviewed by a team of doctors in such a way that each case and its control were as far as possible dealt with by the same doctor. It was impracticable to conceal from the interviewers the fact of whether they were dealing with case or control since in the one case they were interviewing the parents of a dead child and in the other the child was usually living.

It was not possible to interview all parents and some 16 per cent were omitted, either because they declined to co-operate or because they could not be traced. The total number of cases whose parents were interviewed was 1,416.

The interviews involved the recording of answers to a prepared list of questions. These included a large range of questions related to other matters than X-rays so that the questionnaires and the interviews did not concentrate unduly on this question. This provides a degree of safeguard against biased answers. The subjects covered included previous illnesses, diet, and other general matters. The questions on X-rays were designed to discover the kind of X-ray exposure to which the child and its mother had been exposed. In relation to maternal X-rays, the questions permitted distinction to be drawn between X-ray examination during the relevant pregnancy; in the interval between marriage and the onset of the pregnancy; and before marriage. The type of X-ray was recorded so as to permit division into abdominal and other X-rays.

Analysis of the early data showed a substantial difference between the X-ray histories of cases and controls in that 85 cases and only 45 controls had experienced prenatal exposure from abdominal X-ray of the pregnant mother. Stewart and her colleagues considered this result to be so important as to justify its immediate reporting in the medical press. They thus prepared a preliminary note[40] which stated the central finding but did not present a detailed discussion of the research procedure.

These preliminary results received considerable publicity and attracted a controversial correspondence. Those who believed X-ray examination of pregnant mothers to be an important feature of the proper care of many of their patients, and who believed that it led to a reduced mortality and morbidity in mother and child, were naturally disposed to view critically a finding which called the wisdom of the procedure into question. The fact that the data on X-rays had been obtained retrospectively by interview was held by many critics to invalidate the findings.

When the full findings were eventually published[41] in a detailed paper their general nature was confirmed. The relative risk of malignant disease in children who had received substantial X-ray exposure was calculated to be 2·34; i.e. the incidence among such children was calculated at 2·34 times that in children from un-X-rayed pregnancies. The issue of interview bias was discussed by the authors. In their view their data provided an estimate of its likely extent and showed that the magnitude of the relative risk they had calculated was greater than could be attributed to such bias. The basis for this view may be summarized in a simple table prepared from Stewart's data.

Table 7.1

Mother	Abdominal X-ray		Other X-ray	
	cases	controls	cases	controls
X-rayed before marriage	44	26	335	275
X-rayed before pregnancy	109	121	213	184
X-rayed during pregnancy	178	93	117	100

This table shows that there is an excess of cases over controls in respect of nearly all types and timings of X-ray examination. It seems unlikely, however, that X-ray exposure is important unless it is from abdominal X-ray during pregnancy. The excess of cases over controls in respect of all other X-ray situations is likely to be due to interviewer bias, but it also, therefore, provides an estimate of the likely magnitude of the effects of such bias. The excess in such cases is very much smaller than that for X-ray of the abdomen during pregnancy. Thus it seems that although bias is important it does not explain more than a small part of the finding of an excess of abdominal X-ray among the pregnancies resulting in children who died of malignant disease.

The problem of bias from retrospective interviews is important. It arises in the case under consideration because the mothers of affected children will have had occasion to reflect on likely causes and will have rehearsed all the circumstances of the child's history many times to themselves before the interview. They are therefore much less likely to forget such details than are those mothers who have had no reason to indulge in such recollection. A similar difficulty affects attempts to relate circumstances of pregnancy to the occurrence of congenital malformations. Few mothers of such affected children do not recollect untoward events during the related pregnancy. But bias can be considered, measured and allowed for if the investigator is aware of the need.

Nevertheless, the importance of the issue of X-rays and malignant disease—especially leukaemia—and the controversy surrounding publication of the preliminary results, led to a number of other studies being made. Most were conducted on a similar basis but on a smaller scale and their results were equivocal. One study is particularly important, however, because it was prospectively based and produced results which conflicted with those of Stewart. The authors, Court Brown, Doll and Hill,[42] decided to tackle the immense task of a prospective enquiry. The problem is, of course, that in order to have sufficient cases of malignant disease for comparison, the number of pregnancies that must be followed up is very large. Court Brown and his colleagues assembled records of 39,166 pregnancies in which significant X-ray exposure had been received. They collected the data from maternity records of four hospitals in Edinburgh and four hospitals in London. Significant X-ray exposure included pelvimetry, abdominal X-rays, intra-venous pyelography and similar procedures.

Next they collected all data on deaths in children from leukaemia in the ensuing years. They located the birth registration entries in respect of each child, rejecting those not born in the hospitals in their enquiry. Finally they matched the data on the dead children with those on X-ray in pregnancy. They were left with 9 cases of leukaemia among the children resulting from the 39,166 pregnancies exposed to X-rays and in their enquiry. Then they calculated from published statistics on causes of death the number of cases expected among a sample of 39,166 children from the general population over a similar period. This calculated expected number was 10·5. They therefore concluded that there was no evidence that prenatal X-ray exposure predisposed a child to leukaemia although they pointed out that because of random sampling variation their data were too small in number to be capable of disproving a hypothesis that the risk was up to 50 per cent raised.

The negative findings of Court Brown and his colleagues gained a remarkably wide acceptance. Much of this must have been attributable to the use of a prospective design of enquiry as against the retrospective design employed by Stewart. Thus the question of the risk involved in prenatal diagnostic X-rays was shelved and the opportunity to plot another point in the dose-response relationship was for the time being neglected.

The question has now been largely settled. MacMahon,[43] working in Harvard University in the U.S.A., planned an enquiry which avoided most of the difficulties of both prospective and retrospective enquiries and was based on very substantial numbers.

MacMahon investigated malignant disease and prenatal X-ray exposure among the 734,243 children born in the North East census region of the U.S.A. between 1947 and 1954 in hospitals with adequate records. Thirty seven hospitals were accepted as having adequate records of X-ray examination during pregnancy. The records of these hospitals had previously been inspected and considered appropriate. A 1 per cent sample of the births in these hospitals was then drawn by a random procedure. Multiple births were excluded. The X-ray records of these 1 per cent (7,242 records) were scrutinized and 10·6 per cent of the pregnancies were found to have received what was considered to represent whole body irradiation of the foetus.

Records were also obtained of all deaths in children in the region from malignant disease. The birth registration entries of these children were then located and for all births that occurred in one of the 37 hospitals the X-ray records were scrutinized. This trial number amounted to 556 single births. The records of these were mixed in with the 7,242 sample births and those searching the X-ray records did not know into which category each record fell. Eighty-five (15·3 per cent) had received significant prenatal X-ray exposure. The relative overall risk of malignant disease associated with prenatal X-ray exposure was calculated from these data to be 1·42 when the account had been taken of the effects of birth order and of economic circumstances, both of which are associated independently with both leukaemia and X-ray examination. Thus the risk of malignant disease is 42 per cent higher for children exposed to prenatal diagnostic X-irradiation.

MacMahon showed that results from all previously reported investigations lay within the expected sampling variation around a mean value corresponding to the risk calculated from his own data. This work is generally accepted as settling the question and the estimate of the raised risk seems likely to be essentially correct.

The demonstration that a diagnostic procedure may raise the risk of a comparatively rare disease raises many problems. Its importance may principally lie in that it adds additional data to our knowledge of the effects of radiation at relatively low levels and makes it unlikely that there is a threshold below which radiation exposure has no effect. The practical consequences are perhaps less important since it might have been argued in more general terms that unnecessary X-ray examination of pregnant women should be avoided. Nevertheless, research studies have, in the past, been performed which involve routine X-ray pelvimetry. The dangers of this are now established.

The chief interest of the controversy lies in its exemplification of the difficulties of the population study of causes whose effects have a low probability. It also illustrates the danger of supposing a retrospective research design to be inherently inferior to a prospective one, a methodological prejudice which resulted in several years delay in the general acceptance of an important finding. Whenever one seeks to explore the association between an influence which is widely distributed in the population and a possible consequence of that influence which nevertheless has a low probability of occurence, a retrospective equiry is much less wasteful of data and effort than a prospective one. Provided that its difficulties are appreciated and due care is taken to evaluate and allow for the possible sources of error, the retrospective method may be more useful than the prospective.

Chapter 8   Human behaviour as a cause of disease

An important feature of many of the diseases which affect present day society is the extent to which their causes may lie in personal behaviour. Diet, occupation and indulgence in such pleasures as cigarette smoking or alcohol, have for long been known to influence health in a general way and indeed it has been usual for doctors to question patients on such matters when recording a clinical history. What is new is the realization that several important diseases may be more or less directly caused by such influences. What is more disturbing, is that a knowledge of the pathogenic effect of such forms of behaviour has had a generally insignificant effect on their prevalence or on the frequency of the diseases which they may cause.

The study of the influence of such causes of disease and of the factors which in turn determine their prevalence and persistence, falls naturally within the province of social medicine, and there are many examples of such studies. For the present purpose two examples will be used. These are: cigarette smoking and lung cancer, and physical inactivity and coronary artery disease.

Cigarette smoking and lung cancer
Studies of lung cancer and its aetiology are complicated by the problem that the onset of the disease may be difficult to ascertain. Accordingly, incidence rates are difficult to derive and we have usually to base our studies on cancer prevalence or cancer mortality. Since the fatality of most forms of cancer is high and has been relatively uninfluenced by treatment or other intervention, mortality data are quite useful. Many forms of cancer have been consistently diagnosable for some years, and mortality rates therefore reflect quite well the recent history of these diseases in the population. Unfortunately, lung cancer is an exception. Although its fatality is very high, the diagnosis of lung cancer is not always obvious. The terminal

course of the disease is frequently one of recurrent pneumonia and lung infection and this is particularly the case for elderly patients. Since this may also be the terminal course of other chronic lung and even heart diseases, which are very prevalent among elderly persons, the diagnosis of lung cancer may often be missed. This may have been particularly the case before interest in the disease became so intense and widespread as it is today.

Nevertheless, it is generally believed that the frequency of the disease has very greatly increased during the present century. The increase in the annual number of deaths attributed to lung cancer in Britain has been very striking. This is in sharp contrast to the annual number of deaths from most other forms of cancer which has generally declined. The increase in lung cancer deaths has been so marked as to offset the fall in numbers of other cancer deaths and to result in an overall increase in cancer mortality.

It is natural that so striking an increase in the frequency of a disease that has been distressingly resistant to the effects of advances in its treatment should have engaged the attention of research workers. Their conclusion that a substantial part of the increase is real and not the result of improvements in diagnostic techniques is mainly based on analysis of the behaviour of mortality in successive generations. R. A. M. Case, who has made a considerable contribution to the social medical study of cancer, has pointed out that the lung cancer death rate has increased steadily from generation to generation until comparatively recently and that in each generation it increases steadily with advancing age. The steady change between successive generations makes it unlikely that diagnostic changes have been an important cause of the secular increase in number of deaths. A possibility that is of some interest is that the change has been one of site. Since the numbers of cancer deaths at other sites are decreasing while those from lung cancer are increasing, this possibility must be considered. But such consideration is difficult and possibly unhelpful. Whatever was determining such a change would be worth eliminating, since lung cancer is among the most intractable of the common tumours.

Consideration of the possible causes of lung cancer, and of possible changes in its incidence, leads one naturally to examination of local and regional variations in its frequency. It is some twice as common in the larger towns as in rural districts and commoner in some occupations than in others. It is natural to think of exposure to inhaled substances as a possible cause and two lines of enquiry have been intensively pursued. The first has incriminated a number of industrial processes as affecting the incidence of lung cancer; the second has shown the relatively very much greater importance of cigarette smoking.

Since there are many common misconceptions current about the nature of the evidence supporting these latter findings, and since the relevant research well exemplifies many of the problems associated with enquiries into the pathogenic influence of personal habits, it may be well to consider it in some detail.

The possibility that cigarette smoking might be important was first raised by the consideration of the site of the tumour and the likelihood, therefore, that its causes involved inhaled substances. Secular trends in lung cancer mortality and the differential mortality between the two sexes supported the possibility and made it desirable to test the hypothesis that smoking might be involved. Several enquiries were carried out of which the first important one was that reported by Doll and Hill[44]. These workers arranged to be notified of all cases of lung cancer admitted to a number of hospitals. In addition they were notified of two other categories of patient to be used as controls. These were: patients with cancer of the intestine, and patients with diseases other than cancer. Lung cancer cases and controls were interviewed by medical social workers who obtained answers to a list of questions. These related to a number of other matters as well as to cigarette smoking and so far as possible the interviewers were kept ignorant of which patients were cases and which controls.

Analysis of the results from interview of these patients

showed that, on average, patients with lung cancer smoked more than control patients and were less often non-smokers.

Table 8.1

Cigarettes/day	0	1–4	5–14	15–24	25–29	30+	Total
Cases (%)	0·3	3	39	30	21	3	100
Controls (%)	4	9	45	29	11	2	100

The table shows the main results. Although there is a definite difference between the distribution of smoking in the two groups it is quite clear that smoking is common in both groups. The difference, although too large to be reasonably attributable to chance, is not spectacular because smoking is so widespread a habit. No significant differences were found between cases and controls in any other important respect.

This work naturally attracted a great deal of attention. Since smoking is popular, both among smokers and among the manufacturers of cigarettes, and since a substantial tax revenue is raised from tobacco sales, the implication could not be accepted without opposition. Much of the opposition was ill-informed but there were several serious criticisms which may be summarized as follows.

1. Statistical results are always subject to the possibility that an unlikely chance association has nevertheless been found.
2. Answers to questions on smoking may be deliberately or consciously falsified by patients who may fear a worse diagnosis but would like to believe that the symptoms are simply due to smoking too heavily.
3. The association between lung cancer and cigarette smoking may be due to the independent association of each with a third factor; for example, a particular genetic or other constitution may predispose an individual both to smoking and to cancer.

The first criticism was eventually countered by the results of repeated enquiries; the second may be countered by the observation that patients who later turned out to have been wrongly diagnosed as having lung cancer resembled controls rather than cases in their smoking habits; the third criticism can only be effectively countered by repeatedly negative attempts to identify the postulated third factor. But the criticisms are nevertheless important and Doll and Hill considered that they ought to mount another study based on a different design.

A prospective study of the long term experience, with respect to lung cancer, of persons with known smoking habits is difficult to mount. Although lung cancer in adults is much more common than, for example, leukaemia in children, the use of data is inevitably inefficient since relatively few of the subjects of known smoking habits will contract lung cancer. Nevertheless, Doll and Hill[45] tackled a prospective enquiry. They circularized all registered medical practitioners in Britain and asked them to complete a questionnaire on their smoking habits. This included questions on current smoking and on past smoking in the case of those who had abandoned the habit. Over 40,000 doctors completed and returned the questionnaire. Doll and Hill then arranged to be supplied in the ensuing years with all death certificates relating to doctors so that they could compare the risks of death from lung cancer for those smoking different amounts. Analyses of these findings have now been published. They confirm the strong association between cigarette smoking and lung cancer; the death rate from lung cancer is some forty times as great among heavy smokers as among non-smokers and increases progressively with increasing intensity of smoking. A similar study in the U.S.A. by Hammond and Horn[46] on war service veterans produced similar results. The danger associated with pipe smoking is smaller than with cigarettes, while cigar smoking does not seem to carry any risk.

Criticism of these results has mostly come from those in whose interest it is to promote cigarette smoking but one or two serious points remain to be considered. One is that a third factor may still determine both the taste for cigarettes and the occurrence of death from cancer of the lung. New evidence has emerged which makes this unlikely.[47] Seventh day adventists, who do not smoke, rarely die of lung cancer.

Unless a highly pleotropic factor determines religious conviction as well as cigarette smoking and death from cancer, this finding is against the possibility of a third factor which causes both lung cancer and cigarette smoking.

An interesting piece of independent evidence bearing on the question was reported by Kreyberg[48] in Norway. By comparison of data from various published work on the different types of lung cancer he showed that there had been a secular change in the relative proportions of adeno-carcinomas to other kinds. He was able to show that this was most probably due to an increase in the frequency of other kinds while the frequency of adeno-carcinoma had stayed constant. Later he showed that cigarette smoking was associated with other kinds of lung cancer but not with adeno-carcinoma. Thus, it seems likely that secular trends in smoking and in incidence of lung cancer are related.

Since the publication of the work referred to hitherto, there have been many reports of further enquiries; none contradict the association between lung cancer incidence and cigarette smoking and the quantitative relationship between the two is now well established. Edwards[49] has examined the nature of the association between cigarette smoking and relative liability to contract lung cancer. He has shown that the relationship is linear when the logarithm of the smoking consumption is related to the logarithm of the increased liability. He points out that an interesting and paradoxical consequence of this relationship is that if total cigarette consumption were maintained constant by sales promotion methods, and heavy smoking were effectively discouraged, the death rate from lung cancer would rise. If fewer people smoked but consumption were kept constant by heavier smoking among smokers, the death rate from lung cancer would fall. This suggests that it would be better for health education to seek to confine the habit to as few people as possible rather than to discourage heavy smoking. In practice, most official advice has adopted the opposite line.

The effect of the discovery that smoking is the chief cause of lung cancer has been barely detectable. No changes in lung cancer incidence have occurred which could be attributed to a decline in cigarette smoking and the consumption of cigarettes has remained relatively unchecked either by propaganda against it or by taxation policies aimed at discouraging the purchase of cigarettes.

This phenomenon has engaged the attention of research workers who have been concerned to identify the determinants of the smoking habit and to describe and measure the public response to anti-smoking campaigns. Cartwright and Martin[50] and their colleagues have published studies in both these fields and Jefferys[51] has published studies of the development of the cigarette smoking habit in children. Campaigns to publicize the association between cigarette smoking and lung cancer have had the effect that almost everyone has now heard of the association but that only about one fifth of people believe the association to be simply causal. Smokers, more often than non-smokers, reject the causal hypothesis. Many people believe that, provided that smoking is not heavy, there is no risk. The level distinguishing heavy from moderate smoking is set by most people at a level of consumption somewhat greater than their own. It is possible that these attitudes have been fostered by national policy in which heavy cigarette smoking rather than just cigarette smoking has been identified as dangerous, but it seems likely that the tendency to underestimate the risk associated with one's own behaviour has a more fundamental origin. Similar findings have been reported, for example, on the question of what speeds are safe in relation to motor vehicle driving.

A problem is that lung cancer has a low overall probability of occurrence even among heavy smokers. Although most lung cancer may be caused by cigarette smoking, most cigarette smokers die of causes other than cancer of the lung. This raises the question of whether the risk associated with lung cancer may be variable, so that for some people the risk may be very much greater than for others. There are two kinds of evidence which suggest that this may be so.

The first arises from a consideration of recent trends in the mortality from lung cancer in Britain. It seems to have been first pointed out by the Registrar General for Scotland in his Annual Report for 1959, that while the death rate in males over the age of 50 years has continued to increase, the rate for males below that age has not increased for some fifteen years and has indeed shown some tendency to fall. Similar findings have now been reported for England and Wales. At all ages over 50 years the upward slope of the secular rise in age specific mortality has been progressively steeper at progressively older ages. Although the numbers involved at the younger ages are small, it seems unlikely that so consistent a pattern is an artefact due to small numbers. The possibility that it is due to vagaries of diagnosis seems unlikely since it is confined to males; females show a consistently rising tendency for lung cancer death rate at all ages. In addition, no appropriate changes have occurred in rates for diagnostic categories to which lung cancer deaths might alternatively be assigned.[52] It seems that among young males, death rates from lung cancer have reached an upper limit from which they may now be falling while rates for females and for older males have yet to encounter such a limit.

A possible explanation may lie in the notion that the age at which death from lung cancer occurs may be a function of susceptibility, and those who die young are more susceptible than those who avoid death from this cause until later ages or than those who avoid it altogether. If variation in susceptibility represents individual variation in the response to exposure to smoking, then exposure of a population to cigarette smoking would result in deaths from lung cancer occurring at various ages. As the population exposure reached saturation so the mortality at early ages would approach a level at which virtually all highly susceptible individuals were dying from the disease. Mortality at later ages would reach its upper level at a later point in time, since part of this mortality would arise from smoking in early life and would follow its cause after a longer incubation period. A fall in mortality at younger ages might supervene if the proportion of susceptibles in the population fell. Such a circumstance might result, for example, if susceptibility were to any extent genetically determined and high susceptibility were thus subject to lethal selection by its determining death in early life. The speed with which such an effect would occur would depend on the nature of any genetic transmission that might be involved and on the severity of the associated disadvantages. There can be little doubt that a high susceptibility to contract lung cancer if exposed to cigarette smoking would have been a severe disadvantage at any time during the past fifty years. But there can be no reason to suppose that a latent susceptibility would have been disadvantageous during the period of man's history before the widespread introduction of cigarette smoking and there is therefore no reason to suppose that such a genetically determined characteristic could not be both common and simply inherited.

Unfortunately, it is difficult to obtain data which would illuminate this issue. Familial studies are difficult in respect of a disease whose apparent incidence has been subject to changes in diagnostic and nomenclatural fashions. Interpretation of general trends is complicated by the nature of the relationship between dose and response.

Another important piece of evidence that susceptibility may vary has been provided by Kissen,[53] whose work has shown that there may be objectively identifiable differences in personality between those who contract lung cancer and those who do not and that these may be independent of smoking habits. Much more research is required into such possible differences which may permit identification of individuals who may be at especially high risk of contracting lung cancer.

The possibility of a constitutional variation in susceptibility may paradoxically enhance the prospects for eventual environmental control of this disease. Although a general abandonment of the smoking habit seems unlikely, and possibly unjustifiable as a goal, it might well prove possible to persuade highly susceptible individuals to avoid smoking, provided that they could be positively identified. Such identification may eventually prove possible and would transform the outlook for the prevention of this disease.

Physical inactivity and coronary artery disease

Coronary artery disease is much the most important cause of death in Britain today, being responsible for more than one sixth of all male deaths. Apart from its importance as a cause of death, it also accounts for a large amount of disability in the adult population. The disease has a number of different courses and modes of presentation. Essentially, it is a disease of the arteries that supply blood to the heart muscle. Like other arteries, they are subject to degenerative changes which affect the walls and also the lining of the vessels. These changes, which are progressive and associated with advancing age, may result either in a gradual impairment of the circulation within the arteries, leading to chronic degenerative changes in the heart muscle they supply, or they may lead to a relatively sudden occlusion of a breach of the coronary circulation. If a major arterial branch is involved the patient may die almost immediately from ventricular asystole or within hours from gross disturbance of heart rhythm or rupture of the heart at the affected site. If a smaller branch is involved, the patient may either die from progressive heart failure or may recover. Acute occlusive episodes may occur either in persons with no previous sign of coronary artery disease or in persons with a history of disturbances associated with more chronic arterial changes.

The less severe form of the disease known as angina pectoris, results from coronary arterial changes which limit the blood supply to the heart so that increased activity and the consequent rise in cardiac output results in relative oxygen deficiency for the heart muscle, leading to chest pain associated with physical activity.

The consequences of disease of the coronary arteries are various; so also may be its causes. It is easy to see that the heart disease might arise from a constellation of circumstances affecting the coronary arteries, the blood flow within them and the availability of alternative vessels for the supply of blood to affected parts of the heart muscles. The wealth of data that has accumulated on the influences that may determine the disease reflects this possibility of multiple causation.

The frequency with which coronary artery disease has been certified as a cause of death has increased spectacularly during the past 20–25 years. Before we accept this as evidence of a true rise in the frequency of this disease, other possible explanations must be examined. Changes in the frequency with which the disease is diagnosed may be due either to changes in diagnostic fashion or to improvements in diagnostic precision. During this period the use of the electro-cardiogram has developed enormously and portable instruments are now widely in use. Coronary artery disease becomes progressively more frequent with advancing age and the relative proportion of elderly people in the population has increased during the past 25 years.

It is difficult to evaluate the effects of changes in diagnostic practice, but some evidence is available from the records of post mortem examinations that there has been a real increase in deaths due to coronary artery disease. However, it is probably not possible to decide finally on the importance of changing diagnosis of this condition. The influence of the changed age structure of the population is easier to ascertain. Examination of age specific death rates over the period shows that at all ages there has been a 2–3 fold increase. Thus, the changing age structure cannot have contributed more than a small part to the observed increase in recorded deaths from coronary artery disease. However, it is probably less important to note the increase than to observe the present high mortality. About one in every six male deaths is due to coronary artery disease and there is certainly no evidence that its frequency is diminishing.

It is natural that observation of the apparent increase has led to an energetic search for causal factors. Perhaps the initial main-spring of most aetiological research was the clinical observation that there was a preponderance of professional and managerial occupations among patients with coronary artery disease. This clinical impression was early seen to be justified when data on occupational mortality rates were studied. The five social classes of the Registrar General exhibited sharply different mortality rates from this disease, the highest mortality being experienced by Class I and the lowest by Class V. This is the case both for occupied males and single females. However, among married women classified to their husband's occupation no social class gradient in mortality is discernible. In the most recent data, the gradient has become much less steep, since mortality in Class V has increased relatively much more than in Class I. However, the social class gradient for occupied males is still present.

Although it was natural for the medical profession (which suffers a high mortality from this disease) to attribute the mortality gradient to the effects of intellectually exacting and highly responsible work, it was quite early noted by Stocks[54] that within the classes there seemed to be an inverse association between coronary artery disease mortality and the physical activity associated with occupations. Other explanations of the social class gradient have included the hypothesis that the richer diet of the more well-to-do may determine the observed class differences in mortality.

It is the first of these explanations that has attracted most social medical interest. Morris and his colleagues[55] in the Social Medicine Research Unit of the Medical Research Council have intensively explored the evidence implicating physical inactivity as a causal agent in coronary artery disease. Initially they exploited the detailed sickness and other records kept by London Transport to examine differences between bus drivers and bus conductors in the amount and severity of coronary artery disease. They found that bus drivers, whose job is less active physically, not only experienced more coronary artery disease than conductors but also that they were prone to severer forms of the disease. Whereas in drivers there were relatively more immediately fatal attacks, in conductors the disease relatively more frequently manifested as angina pectoris. Before we accept that these differences substantiate the hypothesis that physical activity protects against coronary artery disease, a number of other differences between bus driving and bus conducting need to be considered. For example, it has been argued that bus driving is the more emotionally traumatic activity. However, this is disputable and since emotional stress can, as yet, be neither adequately defined nor easily measured, the matter cannot easily be settled. Another possibility is that drivers differ from conductors either in body build or personality type. In so far as differences of physical shape are concerned, a study of measurements derived from the sizes of uniforms issued, showed that although drivers do tend to be fatter, they experience more and severer coronary artery disease at comparable body builds. Subsequent extension of the inquiry to include, for example, post office delivery men and post office clerical workers confirmed the general observation that those in physically active jobs are less subject to coronary artery disease and experience milder forms of the disease.

National occupational mortality data have been studied by the independent classification of occupations according to the physical activity involved in them and the demonstration that within the social classes the physically more active occupations are associated with lower mortality rates from this disease.

Table 8.2

Death rates (per 100,000) for occupations of differing activity in social classes III, IV and V.

	Activity Light	Active	Heavy
Age 45–54	173	135	102
Age 55–64	528	422	339

Before we can accept this work as evidence of the importance of physical activity as a protection against coronary artery disease, it is necessary to deal with possible criticisms. The first is that social class differences in coronary artery disease mortality are decreasing and do not seem to be demonstrable in data from the U.S.A. This may well be due to changes in the differences between occupations in the amount of physical activity with which they are associated. That there should be a secular tendency for a reduction in the physical activity of occupations seems plausible, although no useful data on the question exist. The absence of a social class gradient in the mortality of married women is particularly interesting since it suggests that the gradient in men may be attributable more to occupational than to other social differences and that for married women, the physical activity of their occupation varies very little whatever the social and occupational class of their husbands. This is again quite plausible, although adequate data are not available on the question.

A more important difficulty concerns the question of whether differences between bus drivers and conductors may arise from the different effect of disease on the possibility of continuing in the job. Bus drivers, whose job is sedentary, may be much less likely to notice early coronary artery insufficiency and therefore be much more likely to continue in their job until affected by a major occlusive attack. Conductors, on the other hand, would be immediately affected by coronary insufficiency and angina pectoris and might be forced to leave their jobs before suffering from an occlusive attack. Against this explanation are the clear differences in mortality in different social classes; it is extremely difficult to obtain new employment in an occupation of higher social class because of physical disability. Social class drift from disease and disability nearly always occurs in the opposite direction.

An interesting further study by Morris[56] and his colleagues was made by sending a questionnaire to a large number of pathologists asking for data on a number of consecutive autopsies subsequent to receipt of the questionnaire. These data showed that the extent of scarring of heart muscle from coronary artery insufficiency was inversely associated with the amount of activity involved in the deceased person's former employment. The condition of the coronary arteries was unrelated to this activity. This suggests that the consequence of coronary artery disease in terms of heart muscle damage may be related to activity but that the arterial disease itself is not. This might be explained if activity influenced the average diameter of the arteries and the number of their anastomotic inter-connexions, thus influencing the likelihood of heart muscle damage resulting from arterial disease. Activity is known to be capable of influencing the average diameter and number of inter-connexions of arteries in other muscles; the blood flow through the muscles of athletes is greater than that through the muscles of non-athletes. No good corroborative evidence for the occurrence of such a mechanism in human heart muscle has yet been provided.

Work on other aspects of social class differences has been carried out in many centres. In particular, the influence of diet has been extensively investigated. This work will be considered in the next chapter as an example of research into the importance of nutrition. Meanwhile, it may be useful to summarize the situation relating to the aetiology of coronary artery disease. Coronary artery occlusion involves the occlusion of a tube. This may occur either in consequence of changes in the diameter or lining of the tube or in changes in the viscosity or rate of flow of the fluids in the tube. The consequences of occlusion may depend on the availability of an alternative route for the necessary flow, and on the extent to which continuing function of the system critically depends on the area affected by restriction of flow. It is not surprising, therefore, that mortality from coronary artery occlusion has a complex causation nor that it may vary markedly in association with a large number of different variables. This, of course, greatly complicates the problem of investigating one of them. In addition, many of the influences that have been incriminated are very widely distributed and vary among people only in so far as their intensity is concerned. All people engage in physical activity. The amount varies from person to person and from time to time for any one person. The distribution of activity between leisure pursuits and occupation may vary sufficiently to obscure the relevance of variation in either. The problems of mounting a study of variation in coronary artery disease associated with total activity have so far proved prohibitively formidable. Similarly, the mechanisms whereby associated variables exert their influence have received relatively little study. We still do not know whether the deliberate choice of diet or of energetic leisure pursuits has any influence on an individual's risk of contracting coronary artery disease.

It is thus extremely difficult at present to promote health education designed to prevent the disease. The situation is particularly disappointing because, in contrast to the situation with respect to lung cancer, we can go some way towards defining the characteristics of individuals who are at especial risk. For example, coronary artery disease is commoner in people with a family history of the condition, in people with diabetes, in people who are overweight, in people with higher than normal arterial pressure and in people with a higher than normal level of cholesterol in their blood as well as among people in occupations involving relatively little physical activity. What we now require is useful, practical advice which we can unequivocally expect to lower the chances of the disease among the identifiably susceptible groups. Thus, prevention of coronary artery disease may depend on our devising simple advice for an already identifiable group of susceptibles; prevention of lung cancer may conversely depend on the identification of a group to whom the simple advice to avoid cigarette smoking may offer a substantial reduction in their risk of the disease. Both diseases illustrate the importance of behaviour in determining the occurrence of disease among susceptible persons and the importance for the maintenance of health, of behaviour adapted to the individual's situation.

Chapter 9 The external environment and health

Although, as we have seen in earlier chapters, the external physical environment is less important than formerly in the genesis of disease, there are still a number of important diseases which depend, to a greater or lesser extent, on such environmental causes. The chief difference between the environmental influences that were important a century ago and those that are important today is that today their control is often technically very simple but socially and politically very difficult. Most of the important pathogenic influences are consequences of things that are socially desirable, such as efficient transport or industrial production, and control of the diseases that they produce may resolve into the problem of striking an acceptable balance between benefit and harm. For example, we could avoid all road traffic accidents by the prohibition of vehicular traffic or at least reduce their severity by restricting all speeds to 15 m.p.h. That no serious person suggests such measures is due to a recognition of the social benefit deriving from motor transport and from the facilitation of travel that it permits. Similarly, we accept that benefits accrue from industrial processes which liberate toxic substances into the atmosphere. The striking of an acceptable balance reflects the general consensus of opinion concerning the relative hazards and benefits as well as the practical limitations of current technology. The balance may shift when new technologies permit or when the consensus of opinion is influenced by changes in the desirability of the benefits or acceptability of the hazards. A good example is the use of coal for domestic heating. In Britain, the advantages of open coal fires are considered by many people to outweigh the disadvantages of the chronic lung disease for which the smoke they produce is largely responsible, while fuel technology has so far failed to secure a better balance between benefit and hazard. The problem is further complicated by general ignorance of the price that is paid for traditional comforts and by the competing pressures of sales promotion for different heating systems. Complete study of the problems of prevention of chronic bronchitis therefore involves not only a simple evaluation of the role of domestic smoke products in determining changes in lung tissues, but also the factors influencing public attitudes to pulmonary disability as well as the technology of domestic heating and insulation.

Thus, research into the environmental agencies that may cause disease is often complex. In the examples chosen in this chapter to illustrate these problems it will be evident that the interaction of environmental exposure with social and personal factors is always a complicating feature whose extent and importance may be variable. The examples chosen are not by any means to be taken as exhaustive but they illustrate the variety of the relevant environmental influences and the complexity of the issues that may be involved in their control. They are nutrition and disease, and atmospheric pollution and chronic bronchitis.

Nutrition and disease

One of the most important features of man's physical environment is the food he eats. In primitive societies the materials of human nutrition depend, as they do among wild animals, on the nature of the surrounding flora and fauna and the resources that are available to collect them. Thus, the basic determinants of human food depend on local circumstances of climate and geography. But among the earliest technical activities of men, as they emerged from a wholly primitive state, were the development of agriculture and animal husbandry which liberated their developers from an otherwise precarious dependence on the local abundance of plant and animal life. Indeed, to some extent, men continue to be partially dependent on this consideration since the success of agriculture and of animal husbandry depends on our success in controlling the prevalent natural circumstances that may often affect them. Today, in the greater part of the world, mankind remains dependent on local circumstances that affect food production since the acceptability of foodstuffs has generally been determined by what is locally available and has remained remarkably unaffected by the advances in trade and food preservation technology which might have been expected to widen the range of acceptable foods.

Food provides the substances that are required by all animal organisms for their continued survival, growth and output of energy. The ready availability of a well balanced and adequate diet varies enormously in different regions of the earth and this, no doubt, explains much of the unequal development of other technologies in different regions. It seems likely that the availability of an adequate diet is one of the most important considerations that has determined the growth of populations and that it may continue to remain so. The mechanisms by which this process has operated are sometimes immensely complex and include, for example, the effect of food availability on the energy resources residually available for other purposes such as the amelioration of the general environment. This mechanism may doubtless operate also in the reverse direction; in an environment where reasonable health is easily maintained the development of food production as well as other technologies can receive a larger share of a community's inventive resources.

In communities where food production is difficult or where it is limited by inadequate locally available capital for its development, the diseases arising from faulty nutrition are almost wholly diseases of under-nutrition, which is often general, although particular dietary deficiencies may dominate the clinical picture.

In many such communities the problems of food supply have become particularly acute since medical technology has reduced the death rate in early life and caused a sharp rise in the numbers of active and growing individuals in the population. It has been possible in recent decades so to reduce early mortality that food resources have become seriously inadequate in many communities resulting in a perilous dependence on a continued avoidance of poor crops. It has been impossible to offset local famine by the use of food surpluses from other regions, partly because of the unacceptability of alien foodstuffs but also because of the transportational and other economic problems of food distribution.

In the regions of the world which either produce enough food for their own requirements or else produce enough wealth of other kinds to permit them to buy enough food, malnutrition occurs for wholly different reasons. Sub-nutrition may occur because of local poverty or because of a faulty choice of diet; although sub-nutrition is effectively confined to children and to the elderly. Over-nutrition which is much more common, has a generally more complex causation and consequences.

In the United Kingdom a continuous survey of population diet is undertaken by the National Food Survey of the Ministry of Agriculture, Fisheries and Food. This survey is based on records of food purchases made by a sample of households. Each sampled household records all food purchases for one week and data on the household size and income are also recorded. The survey includes all weeks of the year except the week in which Christmas falls. Households are selected by a process of sampling based on the electoral registers. Information is recorded on foods obtained free as well as purchased and on the composition of meals and the numbers present at each meal. Meals taken outside the home are allowed for. Data are collected by field workers and analysis is performed annually for annual publication.

General results from the survey show that total food available per head per day considerably exceeds calculated requirements. The wastage is of the order of 20 per cent of the total food available. This is partly explained by food given to domestic pets but cannot yet be wholly explained. Over-nutrition is doubtless an important cause.

Family food consumption varies with region, with season and with economic circumstances. Regional variation is particularly striking. Although total average consumption of nutrients is adequate in all areas, Scotland and Wales have a barely adequate average protein consumption. Variation with economic circumstances is relatively small and average diet compares well with the diet recommended by the British

Medical Association. Variation with household composition is much more marked; poorer households with large families often show inadequate average intakes of protein, calcium and riboflavin.

Rickets in infants

The generally favourable situation is, nevertheless subject to a number of important reservations. One of the more important is the prevalence of vitamin D deficiency in young children. Vitamin D is necessary for the normal growth of bone. Its deficiency leads in severe cases to rickets and in milder cases to less marked defects of bone growth. Vitamin D is derived either from the diet or by the action of sunlight on the exposed skin. In cold industrial areas the amount derived from sunlight may be negligible and children are then dependent on the relatively few foods that contain it. Rickets was once a very common disease among the poorer children of our larger industrial cities. The food policy associated with wartime rationing was responsible for its virtual disappearance. Recently, reports have appeared of its re-appearance among children in Glasgow. The reasons for this are not obvious and require careful investigation. The most important of such investigations have been those of Arneil[57] and his colleagues.

Arneil has summarized the recent history of this disease as showing a virtual disappearance for several years followed by a return in children of a slightly older age group. In Glasgow, the condition was common until about 1938. Its disappearance followed the provision of a cheap dried milk fortified with vitamin D. This effect may have been augmented by the campaigns to popularize cod liver oil and its substitutes and to supply them from child welfare clinics, but this must remain in doubt since only a small proportion of available supplies were taken up (about 3 per cent in 1962) and there are good reasons for supposing that it was not taken up by those families likely to be in most need. Arneil has concluded that fortification of dried milk was chiefly responsible for the disappearance of rickets from Glasgow.

The disease began to re-appear in 1959 among immigrants from India and Pakistan. By 1961 it had begun to appear in native born children of Scottish parents. In most cases the children were from poor households living in very poor housing. Such conditions are not uncommon in Glasgow and the rate of presentation of rickets to hospitals is now approaching ten cases per year. In addition, studies presently being conducted suggest that 'sub-clinical' radiographic evidence of rachitic bone changes is much more common. Some 25 per cent of a random sample of one-year-old children in Glasgow showed radiographic changes of a kind associated with rickets.[58]

Although some of the cases may be due to the recent lowering of the vitamin D content of all fortified dried milks, there are indications that an important cause may be the recent trend towards an earlier change from dried milk feeding to ordinary bottled milk and a 'mixed diet'. In such a mixed diet, adequate vitamin D intake is largely dependent on the inclusion of proprietary fortified rusks and infant cereals, margarine, butter and eggs. In poor homes these may be deficient in the diet. Arneil and his colleagues have carried out studies designed to investigate regional and social variations in the patterns of infant feeding and in the dietary content of vitamin D. Important influences include the urging of breast feeding on mothers delivered in hospital who usually promptly abandon the practice on their discharge and consequently lack advice on the choice of a suitable artificial feed. Another factor is the widespread belief among mothers that proprietary preparations, containing vitamin C but not D, and which are widely advertised on television and by other media, will protect their children from all dietary deficiencies. Arneil has shown that most mothers have no idea what foods specifically prevent rickets. Work on the measurement of sub-clinical levels of vitamin D deficiency and its relation to diet and its determinants is currently proceeding in Glasgow. It involves collection of detailed dietary and social data as well as estimation of levels of biochemical substances in the blood in a large sample of the child population. Experience of obtaining detailed and reliable large-scale data on the diet of young children is generally lacking and special techniques of interviewing are required. Validation of interview techniques can ultimately only be achieved by comparison with objective data derived from weighed sample diets. The task is complex and will not quickly be achieved.

Diet and coronary artery disease

The most important disease that may be influenced substantially by diet is coronary artery disease. In the last chapter we considered how study of social class differences in mortality from this disease led to the hypothesis of its occupational origin, and thence to the demonstration that the disease is associated inversely with the level of habitual physical activity. A number of alternative hypotheses have also been based on observed associations of the condition with socio-economic circumstances. These associations were supported by the observation of international differences in the mortality from coronary artery disease and by clinical experience in countries such as South Africa where socio-economic differences are aligned with ethnic differences which determine quite marked differences in ways of life and in diet.

An important problem in interpreting differences in mortality between social, national or ethnic groups with grossly different economic standards of living is that these differences may well simply reflect differences in the quality of available medical care and therefore of medical certification of cause of death. Nevertheless, enough observations are available on hospitalized illness among different groups and on autopsy records to suggest that variations in the prevalence of coronary artery disease between different groups are quite real. Many studies have sought to correlate mortality from coronary artery disease in different communities with various indices of standard of living. Many of these studies were contradictory even when based on the same data. There are also important objections to the practice of seeking to test a hypothesis by further analysis of the data on which it was constructed. Since the hypothesis that differences in mortality are attributable to differences in ways of life was formulated from consideration of national mortality differences and from subjective impressions of national differences in standard of living, the hypothesis cannot validly be tested by correlation of those same mortality rates with specific indices of living standards. Not surprisingly, studies have shown correlations of mortality with diet, with motorized transport with industrialization and even with the proportion of the population having telephones or television sets.

Nevertheless, there are good reasons for suspecting that differences in diet might account for part of the mortality differences. The most important is that the basic pathological change in coronary artery disease is the deposition of plaques of a material containing cholesterol in the space between the arterial linings and the next most peripheral layer. Since cholesterol is normally found in the circulating blood and is a constituent of most diets, it was tempting to pose the hypothesis that atheroma was due to an abnormally high level of cholestrol in the circulating blood which was in turn due to an abnormal level in the diet. The observation that rabbits, fed on a high cholesterol diet, developed atheromatous changes in their arteries seemed to provide good confirmation of this view.

Studies in man showed that coronary artery disease was particularly common in people suffering from diseases (such as diabetes) in which the blood cholesterol levels are abnormally high. Geographical studies showed that blood levels of cholesterol were generally higher in countries where coronary artery disease mortality was high and lower where it was low.[59] This is particularly true at later ages; levels rise very little with age in less developed countries and rise quite sharply with age in such countries as the U.S.A.

Recently, an important study in Framingham, Massachusettes[60] has shown that the risk of dying from coronary artery disease is related to the level of blood cholesterol. A random sample was taken of adult males in Framingham and to this was added a large number of additional volunteers. Data on the two groups have been treated separately in case the volunteers should differ in any important respect from the random sample. In all, some 5,000 subjects were included and subjected to detailed clinical and biochemical examination. They have since been followed up and more than ten years experience are now available. At the outset, all men with signs of heart disease were excluded. Their subsequent coronary artery disease morbidity and mortality has been examined in relation to characteristics recorded at the outset. The most important associations are with arterial pressure, blood cholesterol levels and cigarette smoking.

At about the same time that the Framingham study was being instituted a study was published[61] of the findings at autopsies carried out on American soldiers killed in the Korean war. These suggested that coronary atheroma was virtually universal in adult American males.

Also at about the same time it was shown that the amount of cholesterol in normal human diets varies relatively little and that it does not seem to influence the amount of cholesterol in the blood.

Despite these findings, there did not seem to be much doubt that mortality from coronary artery disease is closely associated with blood cholesterol levels. These levels are also associated with a number of factors which suggest that cholesterol levels may be related to diet. A striking finding is that among the well-to-do members of the populations of the less developed countries blood cholesterol levels are much higher than among the poor. No associations can be demonstrated between blood cholesterol levels and socio-economic status in studies in the U.S.A. Diets in the U.S.A. do not vary much between the different social classes whereas they vary considerably between people of different socio-economic status in less developed countries. The difference between the diets of peoples with high cholesterol levels and those with low are generally that those with high levels of blood cholesterol have diets containing large quantities of total calories, refined carbohydrates and fat. The fats usually contain a high proportion of saturated fatty acids. Opinion differs as to which of these nutrients, if any, may be responsible for the high blood cholesterol levels, but there is now a large amount of evidence that blood cholesterol levels may be lowered by the choice of a diet which contains a high proportion of unsaturated to saturated fatty acids. Although this may not mean that atheroma is caused by diets rich in saturated fatty acids or that such diets lead eventually to death from coronary artery disease, it does raise the question of whether the lowering of blood cholesterol by choice of diet may offer a means of preventing the development of coronary artery disease in persons identified as at especially high risk by their having high blood cholesterol levels. Unfortunately this must remain an open question at present. The problem is not easy to solve. Men who voluntarily amend their diets in consequence of public knowledge of the available facts may be highly unrepresentative of all men in their liability to develop coronary artery disease; certainly it is likely that they may simultaneously increase the level of their habitual physical activity.

Attempts to settle the question have been embarked upon but they cannot provide complete answers in a short time. One such study, centred on Edinburgh, has involved asking blood donors for a small extra sample for determining the level of their blood cholesterol. Those with high levels have been invited to participate in a trial in which some are given a drug known to lower blood cholesterol while some are given an inert preparation. Their complete co-operation was, of course, obtained. Coronary artery disease morbidity and mortality will be compared in the two groups whose treatment was allocated at random and who individually do not know whether they receive a potent or an inert preparation. Similar randomized blind comparison of actual diets is not, of course, practicable.

It seems likely, as was pointed out earlier, that a disease which represents the obstruction of an artery by blood clot forming on damaged arterial linings, may result from a constellation of circumstances, each of which may contribute to, but not be necessary to, the final outcome. Thus, it seems likely that the association of mortality from coronary artery disease with socio-economic status might be due to several different mechanisms. The original observation has led to a large number of different lines of enquiry, many of which have proved fruitful. We may have reached the situation where further elaboration of all the causal processes is only an academic necessity; many people believe that we have a preventive technique to hand which is practicable and acceptable. This would involve simply the identification of highly susceptible persons by means of population screening for high blood cholesterol, high arterial pressure, high body weight and other associated variables and their treatment by measures designed to reduce these quantities to within normal limits. Such a programme is almost certainly worth a trial as a means of combating one of the most important epidemic diseases of our day.

Chronic bronchitis and atmospheric pollution

As was indicated in an earlier chapter, this very common disease is far from easy to define. Tolerance of respiratory disability varies widely in different regions and between people in different occupations and from different social backgrounds. It is not easy to correlate objective indices of lung function with symptoms of disease. Chronic bronchitis is now generally defined for research purposes in Britain in terms of the clinical history as elicited by a standard questionnaire and consists of a history of 'persistent cough with sputum complicated by one or more chest illnesses necessitating absence from work for at least one week during the previous three years'. This apparently complicated definition works well in practice when it is based on answers to a standard questionnaire. Unfortunately we still lack evidence on variations in the prevalence of the disease over enough groups of the population to avoid the need to study other data based on less stringent definitions.

Studies based on mortality statistics, despite a number of difficulties in their interpretation, have furnished the bulk of our present knowledge of the population distribution of the disease. The principal difficulty in their use is the relative infrequency of the term 'chronic bronchitis' as a certified cause of death. This is partly because the disease more often complicates other terminal illnesses than initiates directly the sequence of events leading to death. But it is also the case that certifying doctors avoid the use of the word 'chronic' on death certificates because it often leads to difficulties over the payment of life insurance benefits. Accordingly, it is usual to analyse mortality attributed simply to 'bronchitis'. It is certain that the greater proportion of such deaths are associated with chronic bronchitis.

This disease, called the 'English disease' but very common also in Scotland and Wales, accounts for a higher mortality in Great Britain than in any other country for which comparable data are available. In addition, whereas in other countries where mortality was formerly high, the rate has fallen substantially (e.g. Japan), in Britain, no appreciable fall has occurred in the last twenty years. It seems improbable that these national differences can be due to differences of diagnosis, although some such differences undoubtedly occur. However, studies are under way (notably by Reid and his colleagues) of the extent to which differences between Britain and the U.S.A. can be attributed to differences of diagnosis.

A detailed study of variation in bronchitis mortality has been made by McKinlay.[62] This established two particularly important associations of bronchitis mortality with sex and age and with occupation and social class. McKinlay drew attention to the different behaviour of rates for the two sexes. Female rates, always lower than male rates at corresponding ages, have been falling fairly steadily since the earliest period for which we have usable data. Male rates have shown a generally downward trend at younger ages, but at ages 50–64 the trend in more recent years has been upwards. The result is that the male excess is greatest at the later ages. Studies by the present writer[52] and by Crofton[63] indicate that the different experience of the two sexes may be accounted for by a greater relative mortality for males of the more recent generations. In generations born since 1881 male rates have been substantially greater than female rates, the difference being maximal for the generations born around 1891 and 1896. These were the generations whose young men served in the war of 1914–18, but since the difference continues in later generations it seems unlikely that war service itself was responsible. It has been suggested by Crofton that the increase in cigarette smoking may account for the trend, and there seems good evidence that it may account for a similar finding in relation to tuberculosis. Another important association of bronchitis mortality is with occupation and social class. The association is very striking as the table shows.

Table 9.1 Bronchitis mortality in England and Wales 1949–53.

Standardized mortality ratios

Social class	Men	Married women
I	34	35
II	53	49
III	98	101
IV	101	123
V	171	154

The important finding is that the association is shown by both men and married women, the latter being classed on the basis of their husband's occupation. This indicates that the association arises more from causes in the general social environment associated with occupational status than in the occupations upon which the social class categories are based. In fact the high correlation between S.M.R.s for men and for married women is seen when individual occupations are examined. The causes of these differences are therefore likely to be localized in the environments shared by men and their wives. The fact that there are social class similarities in the disease experience of the two sexes but differences in the historical trends suggests that more than one cause may be operating.

Among early studies of possible environmentally determined variation in bronchitis mortality was that of Hewitt.[64] He used mortality statistics for the London Boroughs for the pericensal period 1950–52. All the data were taken from official publications—those of the Registrar General for England and Wales, the Medical Officers of Health in the areas under examination and the Fuel Research Station.

Hewitt first confirmed the relatively higher mortality from all causes for males in the London area than for females; S.M.R.s for the two sexes were: males 107 and females 95. The difference between the sexes was most marked in the age range 45–64. At younger ages the mortality of males in London was low relative to the country as a whole—a finding that Hewitt thought likely to be due to selective migration of young workers into the city.

The overall higher mortality for males than for females is substantially due to an excess male mortality from respiratory disease in the age range 45–64 years. Among the respiratory diseases, bronchitis and pneumonia were chiefly responsible for the excess mortality and together accounted for some 4,000 male deaths in excess of the numbers expected on the basis of national rates. Lung cancer and tuberculosis were also more common in London males than in the country generally. This makes it unlikely that any excess is due to diagnostic fashions since these are the four diseases most likely to be confused with each other, and if one were being diagnosed excessively it would be likely to be chiefly at the expense of the others.

Hewitt next examined differences in mortality from respiratory disease among the London boroughs. More than double the national rate for bronchitis was found in the four boroughs of Bethnal Green, Poplar, Shoreditch and Southwark. This concentration of mortality was generally found to be in the east central area. The seven boroughs with high mortality from all causes had the highest mortality for respiratory diseases.

Hewitt had therefore demonstrated:

1. That in London there is an excess of male deaths in the age group 45–64 compared with England and Wales;
2. That there is an excess of respiratory mortality at these ages in both sexes but which is more marked in men;
3. That general mortality in the boroughs is highest in seven geographically clustered boroughs;

4. That these boroughs also have the highest respiratory mortality, amounting to twice that of England and Wales.

Several possible explanations were considered. An important one was that the known social class variation in these causes of death might account for variation between boroughs since different boroughs contain different proportions of the different classes. This possibility was examined and Hewitt showed that it could not account for more than 11 per cent of the total variation between boroughs. Similarly, household density could account for only a small part of the variance.

It is known that air pollution varies markedly in the London boroughs. Hewitt considered these boroughs to be a good subject for examination of this matter for two reasons. First, differences in climate and social factors often associated with pollution are at a minimum in the circumscribed area of London. Second, there were more than 100 pollution recording stations within the area of London.

A refinement introduced by Hewitt was that of allowing not only for the intensity of pollution but also for the duration of exposure. This was achieved by multiplying for each borough the mean sulphur dioxide determination by the proportion of residents actually born in London. This device provides an index of duration of exposure and of intensity, which Hewitt termed exposure to pollution and which he correlated with the S.M.R. for respiratory disease. The correlations were high and showed that about 75 per cent of the variance in such mortality could be accounted for by differences in exposure to pollution. Calculation from these data suggested that with clean air, London mortality from respiratory disease would be halved and total mortality reduced by one fifth.

The problem of social class variation remains difficult to explain. It is no doubt partly due to association between social class and residence in heavily polluted districts, but it seems likely that other influences are important. Recent work[65] has shown that respiratory illness in children is associated with atmospheric pollution and with social class. Attempts to discover any association between bronchitis in adults and respiratory illness in their childhood have failed to yield conclusive results.[66] The possibility that part of the association between bronchitis and social class may be a consequence of the disease rather than causal has recently been raised by Meadows.[67] She showed that patients with bronchitis exhibit a marked tendency to drift progressively into occupations carrying a lower social class. This is an expected effect of a disabling chronic disease. Nevertheless, it is difficult to believe that much of the association is to be explained in this way since it could not easily explain the sharp association of bronchitis mortality in women with the occupation of their husbands.

Other work on the relative importance of atmospheric pollution and other influences in the causation of chronic bronchitis has been published by a number of authors, notably by Reid and his colleagues.[68] They studied mortality and morbidity principally in a single occupational group—post office workers. This has the advantage of largely standardizing social and occupational sources of variation and permitting other correlations to be examined independently of them. The principal sources of data were first, mortality data for the general population, and, second, sickness absence records for Civil Servants. Reid and his colleagues correlated these data with data on overcrowding, population density and atmospheric pollution in 37 areas of Great Britain, grouped into four regions. Indices of pollution were based on data from a survey of regional variation in visibility published by the Meteorological Office.

Mortality data showed a high association between death from bronchitis and atmospheric pollution for both sexes; a similar association was shown for pneumonia deaths in males but was less marked for females. No such associations were shown for lung cancer deaths or for deaths from tuberculosis. Correlations with population density were shown for mortality from pneumonia, lung cancer and tuberculosis and with domestic overcrowding for mortality from tuberculosis.

Analysis of morbidity data from Civil Service records showed the principal associations to be those of bronchitis and pneumonia with atmospheric pollution, and of influenza with domestic overcrowding. Data for postmen and for indoor clerical workers showed attack rates for bronchitis and pneumonia to be similar in areas where pollution was low but to be significantly higher for postmen where pollution was high.

The study therefore confirms the conclusions of Hewitt that bronchitis is specifically influenced by atmospheric pollution.

Although these studies demonstrate the importance of atmospheric pollution as a cause of chronic bronchitis and its relative lack of importance in the case of lung cancer, there are reasons for believing that cigarette smoking may be an important influence in both diseases. We have already discussed the case of cigarette smoking and lung cancer and mentioned Crofton's view that cigarette smoking may be important in bronchitis. Several studies provide a solid basis for the view that smoking may be a cause of bronchitis. Oswald and Medvei[69] showed that the prevalence of bronchitic symptoms was related to cigarette consumption. Edwards[49] compared patients and controls according to calculated total lifetime consumption of cigarettes. The risk of being admitted to hospital with bronchitis is linearly related to total cigarette consumption and is four times as great for those who have smoked 250,000 cigarettes (20 per day for 35 years) as for non-smokers.

Since chronic bronchitis is a symptomatic entity rather than a specific pathologically characterizable tissue change, it is not surprising that the level of its prevalence should reflect a variety of influences. The environmental factors responsible are partly simple and specific and partly factors that are, as yet, incompletely determined. Nevertheless, exposure to the simple and specific factors is not accidentally determined. Social and personal influences play a substantial part in determining individual exposure both to cigarette smoke and to atmospheric pollution. The role of both influences has been clearly known for some time without that knowledge having influenced the prevalence of the disability that they cause.

Chapter 10   Disorders of behaviour

Although the term 'behavioural disorder' has a specific meaning in the context of the diagnostic classification of mental illness, the term 'disorders of behaviour' is here used in the
general sense of mental illness. Such illness is distinguished
from physical illness primarily by the nature of the symptoms;
mental illness involves abnormality of mood or of behaviour.
Diagnostic classification of mental illness is partly symptomatic and partly aetiological. In particular, the major disorders
of mood are divided into the neuroses which are considered as
abnormal reactions to discernible stimuli (e.g. bereavement),
and the pyschoses which generally arise without such discernible stimulus. Some psychiatrists also distinguish a category of reactive psychosis. Within the major divisions, further
classification is principally symptomatic but also partly aetiological both in the case of neuroses and psychoses. As so often
in medicine, the distinction between normality and disease is
not always clear-cut and individual tolerance of mental disability is very variable. The social medical study of mental
illness is therefore heavily concerned with problems of definition of the sick state. A simple but crude operational definition of mental illness may be based on the fact of hospital admission for psychiatric care. Unfortunately, much mental illness is not treated in hospital and the criteria for admission
are, and have been, very variable. Nevertheless, many studies
of the social medicine of mental illness have been based on
mental hospital data, and this may be defended in terms of
the importance of hospital treatment for mental illness which
accounts for about 40 per cent of the use of hospital beds
in Britain. Recently, however, several important studies have
been made of the incidence and prevalence of mental illness
in the community.

The illustrations chosen for the present chapter reflect some
of the current preoccupations of workers in the social medicine of mental illness. They are: the characterization of mental

hospital populations; demographic changes in admission rates; social and family influences in schizophrenia; and mental illness in the community.

Characterization of mental hospital populations
Many studies have been made of the populations of mental hospitals. These have included detailed studies of individual hospitals as well as broad descriptions of national hospital populations. In the U.S.A., several studies have been associated with national population censuses and others have been carried out by the National Institute of Mental Health. Pugh and MacMahon[70] have recently reviewed data from these studies and have commented on the trends which they exhibit. Although diagnostic data were not generally available, the broad trends are interesting. In common with many countries, the U.S.A. has experienced a general rise in admission and residence rates during the present century for all age groups and for both sexes. This is most marked for the older age groups. In the U.S.A., mental hospital residence rates have usually been higher for recent immigrants than for natives and higher for non-whites than for whites. Admission and residence rates are lowest for married people and higher for the single, the widowed and the divorced. In very recent years in the U.S.A. there has been a slight fall in residence rates associated with a tendency to a reduced average duration of stay in hospital. Pugh and MacMahon concluded that this could not be explained wholly or even mainly by changes in the treatment of mental illness. Part of it was due to a decline in the proportion of immigrants in the general population and part of it was due to a change in the relative proportion of patients with chronic organic brain disease.

Recent similar studies in Britain include a census of all patients under psychiatric care in hospitals of all kinds in Scotland. This study[71] was carried out in 1963 as the first step in the establishment of a systematic long-term study of hospital-treated mental illness in that country and will now be considered in a little more detail.

All hospitals in Scotland with beds in the charge of a psychiatrist were required to complete for each psychiatric patient resident in June 1963, a schedule detailing personal identification, demographic data, diagnostic and other simple medical data, source of referral and legal category of the patient. The system initiated by the census permits similar analysis of annual admissions and discharges and permits statistical analysis of the long-term experience of patients resident at the time of the census or admitted or re-admitted since that time.

Among the more interesting findings from the Scottish census were those related to the sex of patients. Females had higher residence rates than males. This was predominantly due to a large excess of females among elderly patients. Whereas one quarter of male patients were aged less than 45 years, less than one fifth of the females fell into this age range. Although about three-quarters of the patients in each sex had a diagnosis of chronic psychosis, the distribution of diagnoses within this category differed between the sexes. There were more males than females with schizophrenia, but females outnumbered males for manic depressive psychosis, involutional melancholia and for the psychoses associated with ageing.

For both sexes, neurosis accounted for a small proportion of all residents (about 6 per cent of women and 4 per cent of men), in most cases the diagnosis was neurotic depression.

The picture for residents contrasted with that for admissions during the same year. Admitted patients were much younger; 67 per cent of admitted males were under 45 years of age and 41 per cent of females. Less than two-fifths of admitted males but about one half of females had a diagnosis of psychosis. Much of this difference between the sexes is accounted for by the very much higher admission rate in males for alcoholism. For both sexes, neurosis was an important cause of admission. These differences between admissions and residents are not difficult to explain. The characteristics of the resident population are determined mainly by the patients who stay in hospital for a relatively long time while the characteristics of the admitted patients are determined more by the patients who are admitted for relatively short durations and who then make way for other patients. Residence rates are the product of admission rates and duration of stay; the great differences in the length of stay at different ages and for different diagnoses account for the very different distributions by diagnosis for admitted patients and for residents. Thus, although psychoses account for the majority of residents, neuroses and behavioural disorders (including alcoholism) account for the majority of admissions.

For admissions at young ages, schizophrenia is the most important diagnosis among the psychoses. At later ages, and particularly for women, manic depressive disease is more important, although in men, its importance is less than that of alcoholism.

Among the more interesting findings is the association of both residence and admission rates with marital state. Married persons have low residence rates at all ages. The highest rates at ages over 25 are for single persons, and single males have higher rates than single females. Residence and admission rates for widowed and divorced persons fall fairly steadily with increasing age. This is very marked for the neuroses and may suggest that the severity of the reaction to bereavement diminishes as age advances. Male admission rates for alcoholism are particularly high among the widowed.

The differences between the characteristics of resident and admitted patients raise the possibility that the two groups may be substantially distinct. Trends in admission rates must be seen against a background of mental hospitals whose number of beds has not altered appreciably for many years and of relatively stable rates until fairly recently for admissions for psychotic diseases. It seems quite likely that much of the recent change in use of mental hospitals has been a consequence of their increasing use in the treatment of reactive rather than psychotic diseases, and that the outlook for hospitalized psychotic patients has altered relatively little. This suggests that long term trends in the use of psychiatric hospitals may depend mainly on the extent to which in-patient treatment of reactive conditions becomes more common, rather than on developments in the out-patient management of chronic psychotic conditions.

Demographic changes in hospital admission rates

The long term history of mental hospital admission rates has been reviewed[72] by Cameron using data from Scotland. Although legal provision for voluntary admission in Scotland dates from 1862 and in England and Wales only from 1930, there is a general resemblance between the histories of admission rates in the two countries. Admission rates were relatively steady from the middle of the nineteenth century until around the decade 1930–39, since when they have risen sharply. There are, however, important differences in detail. It seems certain that the trend in Scotland would have been much more steadily upward had the available statistics included patients admitted to observation wards and to a large Nerve Hospital in Edinburgh which were established in the early part of the present century. The effect of the earlier introduction of voluntary admission in Scotland may have been offset by these additional provisions for non-compulsory admission of mentally ill patients. Scotland has relatively some 30 per cent more psychiatric in-patient accommodation than England.

Cameron examined the trends in admission rates in Scotland and related them to historical developments in the associated health services. He concluded that the rise in admission rates was due to four circumstances; the great improvements in psychiatric treatment that made it worthwhile to admit patients needing therapeutic but not custodial care; the development of a pattern of multiple short admissions for chronic episodic illness; the changing age structure of the population and the greater prevalence of mental illness in the elderly; finally, the trend to smaller families which are less able to undertake the task of caring for their mentally sick members.

Certainly, all studies of historical trends agree in concluding that the great increase in hospitalized mental illness does not arise from a commensurate increase in the occurrence of mental sickness in the population. Indeed, there is good evidence that the frequency of major mental illness may have declined. Such diagnostic data as are available show no marked increase in admission rates for the major psychoses; since the probability of hospitalization for such illness is more likely to have increased than diminished it seems likely that the frequency of occurrence of psychoses has declined. It also seems certain that psychoses arising from such chronic organic causes as syphilis and alcohol must have declined in frequency.

The difficulty of assuming that diagnostic terms remain comparable over a period of many years precludes any more detailed examination of these trends by direct means. Recently, Lowe and Garratt[73] have explored the question by consideration of certain changes in the demographic characteristics of admitted patients. A most striking trend has been the change in the sex ratio of mental hospital admissions. At present many more females are admitted than males. This has not always been the case in Britain and it is still not the case in the U.S.A. In Britain in 1900, as in the U.S.A. today, more males were admitted than females. Lowe and Garratt began by examining national statistics for England and Wales.

The historical trend which has led to a reversal of the relative proportions of the two sexes among mental hospital admissions is complicated by the slight fall in admission rates before 1930 and the sharp rise since that date. The sex reversal had occurred before 1930. In 1901 male rates were higher; by 1911 the rates were approximately equal; since that date the rates for females have been higher. Between 1901 and 1930, admission rates declined for both sexes but they declined less for females than for males. Since 1930, admission rates have risen for both sexes but they rose more for females than for males. Thus, despite fluctuations in overall admission rates, female rates have exhibited a constant rising tendency relative to those of males.

Lowe and Garratt first pointed out that the sex reversal trend was related to age. Before 1901 males had higher admission rates than females at all ages, the rates being highest for both sexes at ages below 35 years and falling at later ages. By 1911, female rates were higher than male rates at ages between 35 and 54, and the rates for both sexes increased slightly with advancing age. By 1931, female rates were higher than male at all ages except the oldest. By 1951, male rates were lower than female rates at all ages and showed a dip in their association with advancing age, so that for males, admission rates were highest in youth and in old age, while in females the admission rates showed a steady increase with advancing age. This has had the effect that the difference between male and female admission rates has become very marked in middle life but much less so in youth and in old age. Combined with the overall trend to rising admission rates, this change in the association of admission rates with age in the two sexes has meant that there has been a large relative rise in admission rates for females in middle life, while at younger and at older ages the rise of female rates relative to male rates has been much less marked.

National data do not permit the question to be taken much further, while detailed local data are not usually available over the long period. Lowe and Garratt therefore tackled the question by different means. They were able to use current data on admissions in Birmingham to explore associations of age and sex with social class and with diagnosis.

Associations between mental hospital admission and social class have been reported from many parts of the world. For all major diagnoses except alcoholism, admission rates are higher for people from the Registrar General's social class V than for those from social class I. The association is most marked in respect of schizophrenia, and we shall return to this special question later in the chapter. In Birmingham it was not possible to relate admission rates to the Registrar General's classes but it was possible to adopt a simpler classification based on area of residence. The wards of the city were divided into three groups—inner, intermediate and peripheral—which reflect social and environmental circumstances as determined mainly by housing data derived from the Census. The inner group is least favoured while the peripheral group is most favoured. Lowe and Garratt found that the inner group of wards experienced the highest admission rates and the peripheral group the lowest. Female rates were higher than male rates for all ward groups but male rates varied much more than female rates between the inner group and the peripheral, their rates being lowest at the periphery. Thus, the difference between the sexes was highest for peripheral wards. The difference was related to age. Among the young and the old, differences were small, both between the sexes and between the ward groups. But in the age range 35 to 64 years, both the sex differences and the ward group differences were marked. At these ages, female rates for peripheral wards were nearly twice as high as the rates for males.

An interesting parallel is thus discernible between the historical changes and the differences between inner and peripheral wards. In the inner wards, as in England and Wales in 1901, there was little difference between the sexes at any age. In the peripheral wards, as in the whole country today, admission rates for females in middle life are considerably in excess of those for males.

Diagnostic information was available from Birmingham, but Lowe and Garratt felt unable to deal individually with specific diagnoses since they were uncertain of the consistency of the nomenclature employed by different psychiatrists. Instead, they distinguished certain broad diagnostic groupings. These were: affective psychoses, other psychoses (including schizophrenia), neuroses, and other diseases. The group of affective psychoses included manic depressive disorder and involutional melancholia. This group accounted very largely for the excess of females over males among admissions of middle aged persons from the peripheral wards. The group containing patients with schizophrenia showed higher admission rates from the inner wards than from the peripheral wards and this was more marked for males. Thus, the association of sex ratio with ward group derives from two causes. First, the admission rates for affective psychoses are higher for females than for males and this is most marked in peripheral wards. Second, the admission rates for the group that includes schizophrenia are higher for inner wards than for peripheral wards and this difference is more marked for males than for females.

It is tempting to press the analogy between the differences that may be seen if the present day is compared with fifty years ago and if peripheral wards are compared with inner wards. But it does not follow that the analogy is explicable in terms of disease causation. Admission to mental hospitals is determined by factors other than mental illness and its severity. Two groups of patients may be particularly likely to be admitted to mental hospitals: the severely ill male patients whose social circumstances do not permit them to remain absent from work without seeking active medical treatment; and the less severely ill women of better social circumstances who tend to demand active treatment for depressive states. Historical trends may well have exhibited analogous changes from a period when only those who could not avoid it were admitted to mental hospitals, to the present situation when much of the stigma attaching to such admission has disappeared especially among more educated people. The causation of the various groups of mental illness and their possible relation to social and historical influences remains largely obscure although, as we shall see, the situation has been clarified somewhat by recent work.

Schizophrenia and social and family background
The observation that the prevalence of schizophrenia is related to social class has been made in many parts of the world and has been based on several different kinds of data. However, most studies have related class to hospital admission for the disease since a diagnosis of schizophrenia is not usually made in patients whose treatment does not involve hospitalization.

Explanation of the social class gradient has been difficult and has involved three different hypotheses. First, it may be that hospital admission of schizophrenics is more probable if they are from an unfavourable social background. On the whole this is unlikely to be the explanation in Britain where the diagnosis is generally reserved for fairly seriously ill patients most of whom have to be admitted. Second, it may be that the disease arises more commonly in people from unfavourable social environments. Third, it may be that the early course of the disease leads to progressive deterioration in the employments available so that by the time a patient is hospitalized he is in an occupation carrying a low social class.

Hollingshead and Redlich,[74] working in New Haven, Connecticut, came to the conclusion that schizophrenics came from lower class families and that social class drift did not explain the association. They believed that the explanation might lie in the different access to prompt and effective treatment that is available to different classes. Their explanations are difficult to accept entirely since at the time of their study there was little evidence that treatment was available which might arrest the usual course of the disease at whatever stage it was applied. It seems likely that their use of the term 'schizophrenia' does not correspond with its use in Britain. In addition, their index of social class included non-occupational criteria and is, therefore, less sensitive to the effects of occupational drift.

In Britain, Morrison[75] approached the problem by using the standard social classes of the Registrar General. He compared the social class distribution of young schizophrenic patients with that of their fathers as recorded at the time of the patient's birth. Patients showed a lower social class distribution than their parents whose social class distribution closely resembled that of the general population. This suggests that the early family background does not play a causal role in determining the association with social class and that social class drift may well explain the association. It is also possible that schizophrenia develops in children who, for whatever reason, have been downwardly socially mobile relative to their parents.

Evidence of the possible aetiological importance of social isolation has been advanced by Hare,[76] who found that schizophrenics more commonly live alone in deteriorating areas such as are found in many city centres. It is still possible that such residential circumstances are a consequence rather than a cause of their schizophrenia.

Recently, interest in schizophrenia has shifted from a preoccupation with the causes of the disease to a concern for the circumstances affecting prognosis. This is because treatments have become available which, while not curative, may substantially diminish the disability associated with this disease. It is now frequently possible to discharge patients from hospital for prolonged periods, after a short initial stay, and subject to the occasional need for re-admission during episodes of exacerbation of the illness.

Cooper[77] has carried out an investigation of the influence of social class on prognosis. He began by noting the contradictory evidence already on record concerning the relationship of social class to duration of stay. His own study was based on all male cases first admitted to mental hospitals from the Bristol area. Diagnoses were checked by follow up of a sample, and Cooper was satisfied that they conformed to the diagnostic criteria in use in the area.

Social class was determined on the basis of the patients' occupations as recorded on the case sheets for their first admission, and the categories of the Registrar General's classification were adopted. Verification of occupation was obtained by interview with the patients or with a member of their households. Patients without occupations at the time of their admission were classified on the basis of the occupation they had held longest.

Cooper's study involved 219 patients. Preliminary analysis showed no association between social class and either marital status or age at onset. Duration of stay was sharply associated with social class and a much higher proportion of patients in lower social classes became chronic patients in the sense that their first admission lasted more than two years. In addition, the total time spent in hospital from re-admissions was also greater for patients from the lower social classes, and the interval between first discharge and re-admission was shorter. Thus all objective measures of prognosis—duration of first admission, total time spent in hospital and re-admission experience —were worse for patients of lower social class.

The patients were also subjected to clinical assessment at discharge. These essentially subjective assessments were nevertheless carefully made and patients were simply classified as 'recovered', 'relieved' or 'not improved'. Patients still in hospital were classified together with the 'not improved' category as 'treatment failures'. The proportions in these categories showed a similar association with social class; 42 per cent were 'treatment failures' in classes IV and V, while the proportion in class III was 24 per cent, and in classes I and II, 8 per cent.

Cooper considered several possible explanations of these findings. First, patients from the lower social classes may begin their treatment at a later stage in their illnesses, and thus be at a disadvantage so far as concerns effective treatment. The arguments against this possibility were mainly that there was hitherto no evidence either that the stage at which treatment commences may influence prognosis, or that patients from lower social classes delay seeking treatment. Their age at admission is certainly not older than for social classes I and II. Second, the co-operation of patients in their treatment may vary with social class. There is little doubt that non-co-operation does influence the favourable outcome of treatment; patients who left hospital against medical advice were generally those who had been graded as 'not improved'. Such patients are more commonly found in the lower than in the higher social classes.

Cooper next considered several particular explanations for the poor prognosis and treatment experience of patients from the lower social classes. The explanations considered included differences in source of referral, patient status in hospital, type of treatment, attitude to treatment and arrangements made for follow up. The types of referral that were considered included private referral, referral through various agencies of the National Health Service and referral from statutory agencies such as observation wards or the duly authorized officer of the local authority. Cooper showed that patients from classes I and II are more often privately referred while patients from classes IV and V are more often referred by the statutory agencies. This establishes the hypothesis that patients from the lower social classes are more likely to be reluctant patients who may delay seeking medical advice for their psychiatric symptoms.

There were marked differences in the proportions of patients who had been certified in the different social classes. More of the patients from classes IV and V were certified. In addition, Cooper showed that certified patients had a longer mean duration of stay and that a greater proportion became long stay patients in the sense of staying for more than two years.

Choice of treatment method was not very clearly related to social class; the principal treatment methods were more or less evenly distributed between the classes. Only two trends were possibly significant. First, the proportion of patients who received psychotherapy was lower in classes IV and V than in I and II. Second, a large proportion of patients in classes IV and V received no systematic treatment.

The patients' attitude to treatment is difficult to measure objectively. However, as has already been noted, more patients from classes IV and V discharge themselves against medical advice. Follow-up supervision of patients after discharge did not differ significantly between the social classes.

Cooper's work has established that prognosis in schizophrenia is related to social class. A later study by the same author showed that prognosis was affected by occupational status and by employment record. Patients with occupations carrying high prestige enjoy a much better prognosis than patients with occupations of low prestige. Moreover, prognosis is related to the family background and is better for patients who can return to a stable family environment than for patients living in isolation. Whether these factors operate by influencing recovery and rehabilitation or by determining the severity of the disease is difficult to distinguish and possibly not altogether a meaningful distinction. If psychiatric disability is defined in terms of socially integratable behaviour, the distinction between severity of disease and rehabilitational success is far from clear.

The controversy concerning whether the association between social class and schizophrenia is causal or consequential is now complicated by the additional possibility that the association of prevalence with social class is at least partly determined by the relation of social class to the effective duration or severity of the disease. Since the prevalence of schizophrenia is difficult to establish except in terms of cases of the disease undergoing treatment, and since prevalence is the product of incidence and mean duration, variation in prevalence may result from variation in incidence or in duration or both. For many chronic diseases, variation in their prevalence is determined much more by influences affecting disease duration than by influences determining incidence. Since duration of disease is often substantially determined by treatment, and since efficacy of treatment may be influenced by as many different influences as affect incidence, the study of the determinants of the prevalence of chronic diseases may be very difficult. In mental illness the situation is often further complicated by difficulties of diagnostic classification and by the fact that the relevant social and environmental influences may be difficult to define and measure.

The importance of family factors in mental illness has often been stressed. Such influences are difficult to investigate quantitatively and it is generally the case that work designed to investigate the causal effects of family characteristics have proved inconclusive unless the family characteristics have been of a simply classifiable kind such as the occurrence of parental loss or broken parental marriage. A major difficulty is that of determining whether familial tensions or disharmonies are consequences or causes of mental illness in the family. Among the more successful attempts to evaluate familial influences in mental illness are the studies of Brown[78] and his colleagues on the effect of family life on the course of schizophrenia.

Earlier work had shown that re-admission rates for patients with schizophrenia were higher if the patients returned to wives or parents than if they returned to brothers, sisters or more distant kin. There was also evidence that prognosis was poorer if prolonged contact with close relatives was unavoidable, as when patients returned to mothers or wives who were not employed outside the home. As a result of these earlier enquiries Brown proposed two hypotheses. These were: that the behaviour of patients deteriorates if they are discharged to a home where strongly expressed emotion is shown towards them; and that relapse might be avoided in such cases if contact with the family was minimal.

Brown and his colleagues studied 128 men who left hospitals in London for addresses in the London area and who were diagnosed in hospital as suffering from schizophrenia. All patients were seen by one of two psychiatrists who satisfied themselves as to the diagnosis, carried out a clinical interview and interviewed a nurse about the patients' behaviour in the week before discharge. Patients were seen again after one year or at the first re-admission to hospital. Patients who were returning to relatives were made the subject of visits and interviews by Brown and a colleague. These interviews were held first with the relatives before the patient arrived home, second, with both the patient and a close female relative living in the home at about two weeks after discharge, and finally with members of the household one year after discharge or at readmission.

Patients were rated before discharge on the basis of psychiatric interviews with patients and with their nurses. Five measures of mental state during the interview were used and five measures of socially embarrassing behaviour. Each measure was assessed on a five point scale. In practice, no patients were rated '5' on any measure. In the analysis of results a patient was characterized in terms of his highest score in each of the two sections on mental state and socially embarrassing behaviour.

Interviews with the family were carried out as free conversations with the patient and his relatives on subjects related to the patient's illness and his plans. On the basis of the interviews the interviewers assessed the situation in terms of five measures. These covered: emotion expressed by the key relative towards the patient; hostility expressed by the key relative towards the patient; dominance by the key relative over the patient; and emotion and hostility expressed by the patient towards the key relative. Each measure was evaluated in terms of a four point scale in which excessive, normal and minimal expression were distinguished. Since such ratings are necessarily subjective a check on reliability was made by comparison of independent ratings made by two observers in respect of sixteen patients. The ratings showed good agreement; only seven of the ninety-six measures involved showed different ratings and only two of these would have placed the evaluated characteristics in different halves of the scale.

At the first anniversary of discharge, or at first re-admission, patients were again seen by the psychiatrists who re-evaluated their behaviour in terms of the same ten items as were used at discharge. On the basis of these interviews patients were divided into three categories: deteriorated, improved, or remained the same.

In respect of behaviour, 55 per cent of patients had deteriorated and 45 per cent had not by the time of their second psychiatric interview. The proportion showing deterioration was related to their mental state and behaviour at discharge.

Families were rated in terms of the results of the assessments of emotional involvement. For simplicity's sake families were summarized as showing either high emotional involvement or low emotional involvement. In families with high emotional involvement, 76 per cent of patients showed deterioration compared with only 28 per cent in families with low emotional involvement. The difference remained if the alternative criterion of re-admission to hospital was used as an index of deterioration and it remained when different bases were used for the classification of family involvement. For example, families may be rated in terms of all five measures of emotional involvement or in terms of various combinations of two or three of the measures. The differences also remained when examination was directed to groups of patients of various degrees of mental state at discharge and also when either mental state alone or both mental state and socially embarrassing behaviour were used to assess deterioration.

The second hypothesis, that the amount of contact with the key relative may be important, was tested by comparing deterioration in groups defined in terms of whether they habitually spent more or less than thirty-five hours in contact with the key relative. The findings were that patients who were severely disturbed at discharge and who were discharged to families

with high emotional involvement deteriorated less frequently
when they spent less than thirty-five hours per week in contact with the key relative. In other categories the duration of
contact was not associated with the proportion who deteriorated.

This work, which has been very briefly summarized in the
preceding paragraphs, is important not only for its findings,
but also for its exemplification of the difficulty of quantitative
enquiry in the area of mental illness, and of the possibility,
nevertheless, of rigorously objective investigation. The original
papers in which Brown and his colleagues published their
findings provide an effective answer to those who despair of
the possibility of scientific investigation of gross disorders of
behaviour in man.

Mental illness in the community
As was pointed out earlier in the present chapter, mental illness
is extremely common and accounts for some 40 per cent of all
hospitalized disease in Britain. Evidence that it is commen-
surately common among patients not treated in hospital is
more difficult to obtain since we have relatively little broadly
based evidence on the occurrence in the population of illness
of any kind. Estimates of the frequency with which general
practitioners diagnose psychiatric diseases vary very widely
and estimates of their occurrence in different populations vary
similarly. Although much of social medical work on mental
illness has been concerned with severe psychotic illness, several
interesting reports have appeared on mental illness in the
community at large.

A particularly interesting example is the work of Martin
and his colleagues[79] who studied the occurrence of neurosis
in a new housing estate outside London. Such a population
presents interesting features for such a study because although
its general demographic features (a high proportion of young
married adults and their children) would favour a low incidence of mental illness, the strains of re-housing and of life
without the support of more distant kin and established neigh-
bours might be expected to promote neuroses. It is also the

case that criteria of qualifications for re-housing include illness in the family and that minor mental illness forms an important proportion of all such disease.

Martin and his colleagues did not attempt to carry out a survey of the population to detect mental illness; such a survey would be open to many difficulties. Instead, they used four indices of the occurrence of illness, of which three derived from records of medical treatment for mental illness and the fourth was based on the results of a direct interview survey in which patients volunteered information on their mental or emotional state.

In studying mental hospital admissions as an index of mental health a particularly fortunate circumstance was the virtual confinement of all such admissions to a single hospital. This ensured not only ease of recording, but also a reasonable consistency of diagnostic standards.

Admission rates for the estate were compared with national rates obtained from official publications of the Registrar General and the comparison was made for different years, for the various ages and for sex, and for different diagnoses. For all diagnoses the admission rates for the estate were substantially higher than national rates and after correction for age differences between the two populations the estate rates varied from 23 per cent to 72 per cent more than national rates, the average for all diagnoses being 50 per cent.

The greater part of the excess was concentrated on women of age 45 years or more. Although such people represented a small proportion of the population they accounted for a large proportion of mental hospital admissions.

The diagnoses for which patients from the estate were admitted to hospital differed in distribution from those in national data. The principal difference was the relative infrequency of psychoses and the relative excess of neuroses. There was a relatively large admission rate from the estate of female patients with neurotic depressive illnesses.

Use of psychiatric out-patient clinics by the estate population was difficult to evaluate because of the lack of comparable national data. The estate made about twice as much use of these clinics as did neighbouring areas.

Consultations with general practitioners were examined from details of records kept by all general practitioners on the estate during a single year. The records were designed for research purposes and were kept in respect of all consultations. Martin took a 1 in 4 sample of these records and extracted details of consultations involving mental ill health. The diagnostic information was classified into three main categories: the psychoses and psycho-neuroses; a group of physical conditions usually thought to have a psychological cause; and a number of ill-defined conditions in which a psychological element seems involved. Martin compared the diagnostic distribution in the estate with that for a national survey of general practice consultations reported by Logan.[80] These latter data were interesting in that they showed considerable variation between practices. This may be due to differences in diagnostic practice among general practitioners or to differences in the practitioners which may determine patients' choice of doctor when they seek advice for psychological symptoms. Consultation rates were generally higher in the estate for psychoses, for neuroses and for most psycho-somatic disorders. For three conditions consultation rates were higher in the estate than had been recorded for any area in the general population. These were anorexia, debility and headache. They were also higher than in most other areas for duodenal ulcer.

Data from a survey of families on the estate included answers to questions on health and use of medical services. Questions included a check list of symptoms which required simple affirmative or negative answers. These were framed in terms suitable for patient recording and the symptoms particularly relevant to the present context were 'nerves', sleeplessness and undue irritability. Comparison of the occurrence of these symptoms with those from data obtained in the National Survey of Sickness shows the housing estate to have considerably the higher rate.

Although none of these indices by themselves could provide adequate evidence of the higher rate of occurrence of mental illness in this housing estate, the findings taken together seem conclusive of the adverse effects on mental health of rehousing of this kind. Additional data on juvenile delinquency and on use of the child guidance services led Martin and his colleagues to postulate the general hypothesis that the conditions of rehousing and of social life on new housing estates are conducive to poor mental health. Subsequent studies for other areas have largely supported this hypothesis.

Mental diseases have only relatively recently been accepted as medical problems and still more recently considered as amenable to aetiological research. Although it seems possible that some of the chronic psychoses (e.g. schizophrenia) may prove to be manifestations of biochemical or other organic abnormality it is nevertheless quite certain already that their progress and the degree of disability they cause may be profoundly modified by the external social environment of the patients. In the case of the common and important reactive disorders it seems likely that their causes will prove to lie in external factors involving the basic processes of social adaptation which are relatively recent in the evolutionary history of the human species and which are subject to continual change. Perhaps because of a greater recognition of the importance of such factors in relation to mental diseases, social medical research in the field of psychiatry has been particularly active and notably rewarding.

Chapter 11   Health and medical care

The most remarkable feature of medicine in the present
century has been the development of techniques which permit
successful intervention in the course of illness. It is no doubt
easy to exaggerate the importance of these developments; it is
important to remember that we still have no cures for the
majority of the chronic diseases and that many diseases pursue
their course towards recovery of the patient largely independently of medical treatment. Nevertheless, it is now frequently
possible to limit the disability arising from disease and often
to influence its course. It is to a large extent in consequence of
these technical advances that most countries have either introduced or plan to introduce systems which help to ensure that
medical care is available to those who require it. For concur-
rently with the technical changes there have been political and
social advances which have led to there being a general con-
census that a community's resources derive from its members
and that these members must therefore be in a position to
benefit from these resources whenever and as they may be
needed.

At this point it will be useful to consider briefly the development of public provision of medical and health care. In England, at least, early developments were occasioned by the
communal interest in general protection. The development of
the public hospital system originated from the laws relating to
the care of the destitute who had originally represented a
threat to society when the dissolution of the monasteries had
unloosed onto the community, bands of potentially criminal
vagrants. Later distinctions between the able-bodied poor and
the rest had largely meant that provision for the poor became
provision for the chronic sick and the confusion between pau-
perism and chronic illness persisted in the provision made for
the poor and the sick into the present century.

Recognition of the nature of infection and the communicability of many diseases led to the development of institutions

to house the infectiously ill. Again, the underlying justification was a self-protective urge on the part of the healthy. Development of mental hospitals arose similarly from the need to protect society from people whose disturbed behaviour endangered or inconvenienced others. The fear felt by the healthy for illness and for sick people is still a potent force in society as witnessed by the problems of obtaining employment for patients with epilepsy and cerebral palsy.

But in the present century there has been a development of the notion that health is a resource in which the whole community has a stake and which it is desirable to maintain and promote. One of the early manifestations of this new attitude arose in Britain at the turn of the century over the discovery that a substantial proportion of young persons were unfit to fight in an overseas war.

Whatever the origins of the present concern with the provision of health and medical care at the community level, the present urgency of investigations into how best to deliver this care to the population derives substantially from its considerable expense. For not only are the drugs and procedures often very expensive in themselves, but the training of modern medical personnel represents a very large investment of resources, which in most countries derives substantially from public funds. It is accordingly politic now, as it was not a century ago, to ensure that available resources of personnel, equipment and materials are deployed as effectively as possible.

Research into the determinants of the effectiveness of medical care has been intensively developed during the past fifteen years. In countries where medical care has been accepted as a wholly public responsibility such investigations might have been expected. But some of the most active work in this field has taken place in countries where there is relatively little organized public provision of medical care. Such research has often been described as operational research into the functioning of the medical services and much of it has naturally been directed towards local or short term management problems or to studies of the basis for the distribution of public resources. But the recognition that the quality and availability of medical care are among the determinants of community health has led to many studies in which medical care has been one among several factors that have been examined as influencing the incidence or prevalence of particular diseases.

In the present chapter, a number of studies will be considered as examples of research in this general field. They will be grouped under three heads; studies of the training and use of doctors, studies of the organization and deployment of medical care, and studies of the factors that influence the uptake of medical care by those in need of it.

Training and use of doctors

The scientific study of medical schools and of medical students has been developing over a number of years. The sources of an interest in this field are various and have determined a number of different approaches and have involved investigators from several different fields. Sociologists have generally come to such studies either from a background of the developing sociological interest in the functioning of complex organizations of which educational institutions form a particularly interesting example, or from an interest in the processes by which the human species develops the behaviour patterns which characterize the adult as distinct from the child society, an area in which the study of educational processes forms an especially important part. In addition, there has been a long interest in the sociology of the professions and in the professional training institutions in which many of the characteristics of professional attitudes and behaviour are consciously or unconsciously fostered. Educationalists have interested themselves in medical education as an almost unique example of educational processes in which attempts are made simultaneously to develop a technology and a characteristic culture against an academic background embracing the very different approaches of the natural and the behavioural sciences. Research by medical men into medical education has arisen principally from a general awareness of its imperfections and a desire to base projected improvements on some better principle than the resolution of competing professorial interests.

These diverse motivations for enquiry into medical education have determined three broad lines of approach. At the simplest level there has been research into the curricular content of courses of instruction and into the relative effectiveness of various tuitional and examinational techniques. Much of this work has been complicated by the absence of any consensus of opinion concerning the objectives of medical education and how their achievement might be evaluated. It is usually impracticable to study the health of the patients of doctors subjected to different curricular or tuitional procedures. Such attempts as have been made to evaluate postgraduate performance in relation to educational methods have generally employed some such index as postgraduate examination success or attendance at postgraduate courses. But in many cases the objectives have been even more limited and have related tuitional techniques to examination success or have compared the rankings obtained by candidates in alternative examinational procedures. By such means, for example, it has been established that multiple-choice examination techniques can be made to produce similar results to those from conventional essay-question examinations. It is difficult to say whether this should be greeted with enthusiasm or the reverse.

Sociologically based research has generally concerned itself with two main areas of interest. The first has been the study of the medical school as a social institution and the second has been its relation to the profession of medicine itself. Studies of the former type belong to sociology rather than to social medicine but they have been of interest in showing that different schools of medicine (in the U.S.A. at least) may have very different student cultures. Studies from Kansas,[81] for example, revealed the medical student in the role of an immature person engaged in a difficult trial by ordeal by which he might eventually qualify for admission to the post-initiation ranks of the medical profession itself. In contrast, other studies[82] have shown the medical student more as a junior colleague of his professors whose role was that of being under guidance from more senior persons.

Elements of both kinds of society can be observed in British medical schools, although many would feel that identification with the role of the doctor was rare among students. As Martin[83] has pointed out, British students are much younger than those in American medical schools and their educational background has been more narrowly specialized. The more hierarchical structure of British hospital organization and the higher value generally placed in Britain on prolonged experience may also contribute to a defensive sub-culture. Martin suggests that such a culture may explain the lack of competitiveness notable in British medical students who see themselves solidly ranged against an irrational examination system.

Studies of the relationship between medical education and medical practice have mostly concerned themselves with quite limited objectives. An interesting[84] and important study was that of Peterson and his colleagues who included in a general study of medical practice an analysis of the association of current standards of practice with performance in medical school. They found that above average performance in practice was associated with above average performance as a student, and that a concern for the social and emotional content of medical practice was most marked in those whose technical skills and knowledge were above average. Interestingly, they were able to show that the influence of medical school performance on practice was most marked in recent graduates and diminished with increasing age of the practitioners. It is not possible to decide whether this is due to the diminution of the educational influence as it becomes more remote in the past or to the more marked effect of education in relatively recent times.

From the point of view of social medicine, studies of the origins of the medical student and of how his educational experience affects his choice of medical career are of particular interest. One major study carried out in Britain has been sponsored by the Association for the Study of Medical Education, and reported by Martin and his colleagues.[85]

This study was based on an attempt to obtain responses to a questionnaire circulated to some 10,000 British medical students in 1961. The response was good and 94 per cent of all students returned completed questionnaires, the total number being 9,356 replies from twenty-four British and one Irish school. The questions covered the educational and social background of the students, their reactions to their training, their study habits, their leisure pursuits, their attitudes to their profession and their intended choice of career. The study was designed so that it may be continued over a period, and relatively few of the results have been published so far. However, private and limited communication of the results permits a brief account of some of the findings.

The social origins of these British medical students are of some interest. More than half have fathers in managerial or professional occupations and only one seventh are the sons or daughters of manual workers. One fifth of the students have fathers who are themselves doctors. The maintenance of a professional sub-culture is of course greatly facilitated by this relative homogeneity of family social background.

Although there are some variations between the individual medical schools, the predominant picture of a recruitment largely from the professional classes is quite clear. In this respect, the similarity with American medical schools is interesting. Despite the much greater financial support available from public sources, the British medical profession is succeeding no better than its U.S. counterpart in recruiting from the whole range of the community. Martin has suggested that an important reason may lie in psychological and cultural factors which prevent the medical profession being seen as an attainable goal for young men and women from working class backgrounds, although other professions have undoubtedly become much more attainable in recent years. It is also likely that social selection plays a part in the processes governing admission to medical schools. Since the informal interview plays a large part in these processes, it is likely that the image against which applicants are being judged is one which resembles the selectors' own view of themselves as professional men. Evidence that this is so is difficult to obtain, but the concentration of students from the higher social classes in the medical schools generally believed to be particularly desirable suggests that the selection process is socially biased. Few medical schools use objectively based measures of aptitude as ultimate criteria for selection and the opinion is often expressed by medical teachers that such objective tests are less useful than informal judgements of candidates' suitability for the profession.

Among a very large number of aspects of medical education studied in this enquiry, the determinants of a choice between the various careers open to the medical graduate is of particular interest. This is because of the substantial number of graduates who eventually accept careers that were not initially their first choice. In the medical student enquiry, data are at present restricted to the student's statement of his choice, although the investigators plan to collect data which will permit an examination of actual careers entered and a comparison with earlier preferences.

A firm choice of career is made quite late, and even in the final year only a little over a quarter of the students have arrived at a firm decision. Preferences are expressed at an earlier stage, however, and it is interesting to examine how these are arrived at and how they change. The most striking findings are the consistent preference at all stages for a career in hospital medicine, the low rank accorded to research careers, and the slow increase during the medical course in the proportion expressing a preference for general practice. Martin has summarized the situation in what he describes as a possibly misleading over-simplification—'the medical student in his first year at medical school wants to be a surgeon, the student commencing his clinical studies sees himself as a physician, while the man approaching his final examinations has settled for general practice.' These changes may well reflect the operation of an improving understanding of the actual distribution of careers within the profession, and an accommodation to the inevitable effects of demand. On the other hand, they may simply reflect the relative effects of the training periods involved in the various careers and the maturing students' wish for marriage and family life which may seem more compatible with a choice of general practice.

These studies of the early determinants of the market in medical manpower have a fundamental long term significance in the planning of medical services. In the shorter term, there is a serious shortage of medical manpower in many countries which might be at least partially remedied if more effective use could be made of women medical graduates. A recent study of the problems has been made by Jefferys and Elliott.[86]

In this study, sponsored by the Medical Practitioners' Union, a questionnaire was sent to 11,594 women whose names were listed in the Medical Directory, 1960, or on the new lists of registrations for 1960, 1961 and 1962, and who were not listed as retired, or resident outside the U.K. Replies were eventually obtained from 75 per cent of those who received questionnaires. The possible significance of the high rate of non-response was considered by the authors wherever it seemed relevant.

The questions related to marital state, number of children, employment history and present employment as well as to obstacles to employment and how they might be overcome. An interesting question was whether they had married a doctor and 57 per cent of the married women replied that they had.

Just under half of the women were working whole-time while just under one fifth were not working. About one third had part-time work. Of those working whole-time, two-fifths were in general practice, two-fifths in hospital practice and the majority of the remainder were in public health practice. Of those in part-time employment, two-fifths were in general practice, about one quarter in hospital practice, another quarter in public health, while about one third were in other employments. Since part-time workers frequently had more than one employment these proportions do not relate to exclusive employment within these branches.

The proportion not working varied with age, being least in the age group 45 to 54 and higher at both younger and older ages. The authors attribute the fall in employment at older ages to health reasons and the lower level of employment at younger ages principally to maternity.

Over 90 per cent of the single women doctors were working; mostly whole-time. A similar proportion of the widowed and divorced were working although rather more of these were in part-time work. The lowest proportion in work was among married women with children under five years, although one sixth of these were working whole time and nearly half were working part-time. Married women whose children were over five years old or who were without children were almost equally likely to be working, but in both cases were much less likely than single women and more likely, if working, to be in part-time work.

Although these results are far from surprising, the questions concerning the desire to work and the reasons for not working produced some unexpected results. Over three-quarters of the younger women who were not working stated that they wished to work, and over one third of those in part-time work stated that they would do more work if it were available. Of those who would have liked to work, over half gave as a reason for not working the lack of suitable employment opportunity. Few women stated that their husbands disapproved of their working and such disapproval does not seem a significant reason for not working. Of the married women who answered the question, those who were working often felt it financially worthwhile; those who were not working more often felt it not financially worthwhile.

It seems clear that the principal reasons for the under-employment of women medical graduates are marriage and maternity and the lack of suitable work which would permit a combination of professional and family satisfactions. It is difficult to estimate the future availability of suitable work since it must depend on policy decisions, but these should rest on an appraisal of the likely demand for employment and of how it might be modified by the availability of such work.

Trends in marriage and maternity among women medical graduates were examined by Jefferys and Elliott. The proportion of women doctors who marry is less than that in the adult female population. But analysis of the proportions married at each age group showed that for women doctors, as for all women, there has been a trend towards marriage which has been more marked for the doctors. Although the age at marriage has been falling for the general population of women, it has risen in recent years for women doctors. This is mainly because the age at qualification has been rising while the proportion who marry before qualification remains small. Despite this somewhat later age at marriage, the fertility of married women doctors is higher than that for wives of professional men in general or than the general population of women. There are also indications that the fertility of married women doctors may be rising; the proportion of those aged 30 to 39 having two or more children was higher than for those aged 45 to 49. It seems likely that the combination of late marriages and high fertility will be especially likely to result in an interrupted career which in its turn may lead to partial or complete abandonment of medical work if suitable steps are not taken to make it easier for married women doctors to find suitable work.

Such studies of the recruitment, training and subsequent employment of medical personnel may eventually contribute to the formation of a coherent social policy in relation to manpower for the medical services. If and when they do, they may provide the basis for a more effective use of our resources and would be likely therefore to contribute substantially to the promotion of community health.

Organization and deployment of medical care
There remain few countries in the world today where the provision of health and medical care is left substantially to private arrangements made between doctors and patients and where the costs of medical care are met primarily from the resources of each consumer at the time of use. In most countries, substantial proportions of the population have the costs of their medical care met on a communal basis. This may be by means of private insurance systems, state sponsored insurance or by public provision of a comprehensive service. In some countries (e.g. the U.S.A.) more than one type of system may be in operation. In Great Britain, as in a few other countries,

medical and health care is a public responsibility, the cost of which is almost wholly met from public funds deriving from general taxation.

The advantages of such a system are chiefly the convenience to the user and the accessibility of medical care than can in principle be achieved. The expected advantages of closely controlled costs and a rational planning of medical care in terms of defined needs cannot generally be said to have been realized. The reasons for the lack of success in these respects have only recently begun to be objectively investigated since it is only relatively recently that it has been conceded that such studies are either proper or likely to be rewarding. Such studies may be approached by epidemiologists as a natural development of their concern with the determinants of community health, by economists as a part of their concern with the deployment of public resources or by students of administration as an example of a novel extension of administrative responsibility into areas traditionally governed by private inter-personal transaction. In any case, since the results of such studies are relevant to the maintenance and promotion of community health, it is a natural function of departments of social medicine to systematize the findings.

The organization of medical care in Great Britain is of particular interest because the British National Health Service was among the first to attempt to deploy medical care as a public resource available to all residents in need of it without qualification or barrier. For this reason it may be regarded as a prototype from which other services may be developed and whose operation is therefore the subject of intense scrutiny.

Although the service bearing the title of the National Health Service came into being in 1948, public provision of medical care had been developing for several centuries before that, and in the present century had been extensively promoted before 1948. The hospital service had a complex origin in which public provision for the chronic sick, the sick poor, the dangerously infectious, the dangerously mentally ill and finally the acute sick had developed alongside a voluntary hospital system based essentially on charity. During the war of 1939 to 1945 the hospital services had been nationally organized to meet the contingencies of wartime emergency and the National Health Service essentially took over an existing organization. The public health service had grown up in response to the recognition of the communal risks of infectious disease, and its personal health services (maternity and child welfare and school health services) had been developed because of an increasing recognition of the public value of a healthy force of young adults. The latter services had assumed the major part of the responsibility for the promotion of health and the treatment of minor illness in children and mothers. From 1911, National Health Insurance had provided a financial base for general practitioner care for insured workers (although not for their families) and had thus ensured such care for the majority of adult males. Thus, by 1948 the major part of the cost of the health and medical care provided was met from communal sources and even private medical care was heavily subsidized by the availability of resources developed in the public sector and by the heavy public subsidization of the education and training of medical and nursing personnel.

The actual organization of medical care in 1948 and its subsequent development under the National Health Service reflects the piecemeal growth of the service from many origins. The particular features that have seemed most unfortunate have been the separation of the preventive and curative services, the sharp distinction between hospital and domiciliary practice and the resulting triplication of services such as maternity care which involve both prevention and therapy and domiciliary as well as hospital care. This compartmentalization of the service is not only confusing for patients and a source of dissatisfaction for doctors, but it leads to discontinuity in the care of chronic illness and a consequent impairment of rehabilitation. The duplication or triplication of services has led to professional feuds and has aggravated the prevalent shortage of staff which derived from the attempt to man a more comprehensive system of care without a commensurate increase in the numbers of doctors and nurses.

It is now generally recognized that, despite its obvious

virtues, the National Health Service is in need of drastic redesign and that such redesign ought to be preceded by an intensive study of the problem of delivering comprehensive medical care in the context of present and predictable patterns of morbidity and the availability of personnel and other resources.

In other countries, research into the problems of providing medical care has taken two main forms. First, studies have been made of medical needs and how effectively they are being met by existing services. Second, experimental studies have been made in which alternative systems have been established and their relative effectiveness compared. In Britain, experimental studies have largely been precluded by the rigid statutory basis of the health service administration but many proposals have been made for experimental developments.

Evaluation of medical care has hitherto been made in terms of relatively crude indices such as death rates or mean durations of stay in hospital, and areas or systems have been compared in respect of such indices. Somewhat more sophisticated methods have involved the establishment of simple criteria of good medical care in a particular context. For example, the frequency with which patients with diabetes have retinal examinations for the detection of diabetic retinopathy, or the frequency with which pregnant mothers have urine analyses, for sugar and albumen, or blood examinations for rhesus blood groups, might be used as indices of the quality of medical care.

It may be useful to illustrate these themes by considering actual studies from the relatively restricted field of maternity care. This field has been chosen not only because it is particularly important but because it is familiar to the author.

Although mortality from causes arising before, during and shortly after birth has steadily fallen during the present century, there remain considerable differences in the levels experienced in different countries and among different sections of the population. Perinatal mortality rates in the United Kingdom are considerably higher than those in some other European countries, and in Scotland they are higher than in

England and Wales. Within Scotland, as elsewhere, there are marked differences between urban and rural areas, and between North and South. However, much the most marked association is with the social class of the parents.[52] Class differences vary for different causes of death and perhaps surprisingly, are very marked for stillbirths. What is disturbing is the persistence of the social class gradient in this early mortality despite a general tendency for mortality in all classes to have declined during the past twenty years.

The class gradients are marked for causes of death, such as birth injury, asphyxia and prematurity, where it is reasonable to expect that the quality of maternity care may influence the outcome. That good maternity care is not equally distributed is suggested by the social class differences in the proportions delivered at hospital or at home. Mothers from the classes whose domestic circumstances are usually least suitable for domiciliary delivery are more frequently delivered at home.

These general observations prompted a special study of maternity care in Glasgow where the mortality rates are particularly high.[4] The first stage in the study involved the design of a new Health Visitor record so that relevant data might be recorded in a form suitable for analysis. All births in the city were included.

Analysis of the data for births in 1963 was concerned principally with ante-natal care, place of delivery and risk of perinatal death.

The first problem to be considered was the effect of indications for hospital delivery on the actual place of confinement. Indications for hospital delivery were grouped into three categories distinguishing those based on past obstetric history (category 1), those based on social circumstances (category 2), and those arising from complications of the current pregnancy (category 3). The indications were those generally accepted by obstetricians as favouring the choice of hospital confinement. Category 3 indications have the most marked effect in determining hospital confinement; 88 per cent of those with such an indication were delivered in hospital compared with 63 per cent of those without. Category 1 indications were next in importance; 75 per cent of those with such an indication were delivered in hospital compared with 63 per cent of those without. Category 2 indications had a negligible effect; 71 per cent of those with such an indication being delivered in hospital and 69 per cent of those without.

Of course, many women had indications in more than one category and a number had indications in all three categories. Analysis showed that where an indication in either category 1 or 3 was present, the addition of an indication in category 2 had a negligible effect in securing hospital delivery. Where indications in categories 1 and 3 were absent an indication in category 2 exerted a slight effect but the hospital delivery rates remained well below the average for the total population. It is important to note that at least one indication for hospital delivery was present in respect of 92 per cent of the population.

Some of the individual indications are of particular interest. Social class, for example, had little effect on place of delivery but perinatal mortality showed the usual association with social class. Class differences in perinatal mortality were more marked for domiciliary deliveries than for hospital deliveries, which may be attributed either to the effect of hospital delivery in reducing avoidable deaths or to the possibly more effective selection of women at high risk in the more favoured classes.

Domestic circumstances were described in simple terms in the individual records. Two items were used in the analysis; presence of a fixed bath and presence of a W.C. Absence of either of these amenities is associated with a very slightly higher hospital confinement rate. Nevertheless, more than a quarter of deliveries to mothers living in homes which lack these amenities are conducted at home. Among women with five or more previous births, delivery is more likely to be at home if the home lacks these amenities than if it possesses them.

Perinatal mortality exhibited the usual association with birth order, being high in first births and in fourth and higher orders. The rate was especially high among first births occurring at home. Mortality was also associated with the numbers of previous stillbirths being some eight times greater for children of mothers with two or more stillbirths than for mothers with no previous stillbirths. Despite this, the likelihood of hospital delivery was only slightly related to a previous history of stillbirth and one sixth of all mothers with a history of two or more stillbirths were delivered at home.

Perinatal mortality also increases with the number of previous miscarriages. Nevertheless, a history of previous miscarriage does not increase the chances of hospital delivery; indeed, a history of one previous miscarriage was associated with a lowered likelihood of delivery in hospital.

The proportions delivered in hospital decreased slightly with delay in starting ante-natal care, especially when this was delayed beyond the thirtieth week of pregnancy. Perinatal mortality was high in this latter group but was also high among those who started ante-natal care very early (before the tenth week). This may be because so early a start to ante-natal care is occasioned by an awareness of special factors associated with a high risk of foetal death.

Ante-natal care is generally believed to be an important factor in safeguarding the foetus as well as its mother. Broadly, three sources of such care are available—the maternity hospital, the local authority clinic, and the general practitioner. Ante-natal care may be received from any or all of these sources or from none. To a large extent the source of care is determined by the choice that is made about place of confinement and in some cases the place of confinement may be determined by the source of ante-natal care.

Generally, if ante-natal care is provided by the general practitioner only it may be concluded that a domiciliary delivery was intended. This was confirmed in the Glasgow study by the fact that only 28 per cent of such women were delivered in hospital, and by the high perinatal mortality in the children of these women who represent those in whom complications of pregnancy determined a change of decision about place of confinement.

Women who had their ante-natal care from the hospital only were nearly all delivered in hospital (96·7 per cent) and

had a low perinatal mortality (37·0 per 1,000 births). Women
who had care from local authority clinics only were also
mostly delivered in hospital (89·4 per cent) and had a very
low perinatal mortality (29·6 per 1,000 births). The difference
in mortality in these two groups may be due to the selection
for hospital ante-natal care of those with known conditions
involving risk to the foetus.

Ante-natal care influences not only the health of the mother
and child but also the place of delivery. Before the National
Health Service such care was principally provided by the local
authority clinics or the maternity hospitals, since relatively
few women had a general practitioner whose services could
be afforded. In England (but not in Scotland) the majority of
deliveries were conducted by midwives in the patients' homes
and no doctor was actually present. This is still substantially
true for domiciliary births in England although the proportion
of mothers using the local authority ante-natal clinics has
declined since 1948. Richards and Lowe[87] have pointed out
that for the decade following the introduction of the National
Health Service the steady decline in the stillbirth rate that had
occurred before then was arrested. They suggested that this
might have been due to a decline in the quality of ante-natal
care when such care was substantially transferred from the
local authority clinics to the general practitioners. These
authors reached their conclusion after failing to find an alternative explanation for the phenomenon.

The availability of three sources of ante-natal care and the
differences between them in standards of training and available
equipment as well as their effect on place of delivery makes
it important to assess their relative functions and to discover
how effectively cases are allocated between them. Although
few such studies have yet been reported there are several in
progress and it is becoming clear that an important determin-
ant of the quality of maternity care is the choice exercised by
the mother. Such a conclusion, which accords with clinical
experience, suggests the need to analyse more precisely the
determinants of the attitudes that underlie the mothers' choice,

if we are to ensure a more effective use of the different virtues
of the different patterns of care.

The uptake of medical care

Studies of the formation of those attitudes which influence the
uptake of medical care represent a particular example of a
general contribution which sociological enquiry may make to
social medicine. As has earlier been suggested, the level of
community health may be affected by prevalent public attitudes to general or specific health measures, to personal
behaviour or to tolerated levels of disability. It can similarly
be affected by attitudes which determine the use of medical
care and the effectiveness of the relationship between the personnel of the health and medical services and the public they
are designed to serve. Studies of this kind have not been
numerous and many of them have lacked either a clear per-
ception of the medical problems or an understanding of the
sociological issues involved. However, a few relatively simple
studies have been published which illustrate the importance of
public attitudes in the effective delivery of medical care to
the community. One problem will be used to illustrate this
theme; the characteristics of women making use of cytological examination for the detection of early uterine cervical
cancer.

The development of cytological techniques which have been
claimed to be capable of detecting a pre-malignant phase in
the development of cancer of the uterine cervix seemed to
promise a break-through of considerable importance in the
preventing of a common form of cancer. If this disease can
indeed be detected in a pre-symptomatic and pre-malignant
phase of its course then it would seem that it should not be
difficult to effect a marked reduction in its mortality. Unfortunately, cancer of the cervix is not distributed randomly in
the population (few diseases are) and the distribution of the
disease provides a few clues to the difficulty of an effective
application of screening procedures. The disease is commonest
in women from the poorer socio-economic groups and in
women who have had more than the average number of

children. Like most forms of cancer, its incidence increases
with advancing age.

The test procedure involves a vaginal examination and
the scraping of the lining of the cervix to obtain cells which
may be examined microscopically. The procedure is painless
and simple but requires skilled performance if it is to yield
satisfactory results. It could not easily be performed other than
in suitable premises and it is thus usually necessary for women
to attend an examination centre.

MacGregor and Baird[10] reported a study of a cervical
screening campaign in Aberdeen. Having previously found
that a campaign based on routine testing of women attending
gynaecological out-patient departments yielded about one per
cent of positive cases, they gradually expanded the service to
include women attending Family Planning Clinics and the
patients of selected general practitioners. At an early stage it
was decided to investigate three selected practices to identify
the important determinants of the level of response to a
campaign.

The practices chosen for the study included one in which
a high degree of enthusiasm was manifest, one in which enthusiasm was somewhat less and a third in which the effect
of enthusiasm was deliberately countered by a request to the
practitioner to refrain from active participation in getting
patients to attend.

A suitable letter was composed and copies sent to all
married women aged 25 to 60 years. Each letter was signed
by the patient's own doctor and contained a brief account of
the purpose and nature of the test and a request to attend at
the doctor's own consulting room for examination by a woman
doctor. A second letter was sent in most cases where no reply
was received to the first.

Of 5,340 women invited to attend, 2,683 were actually
examined and 24 were found to have abnormalities. Of these,
18 were considered to have pre-invasive or invasive cancer
and one had a clinical cancer.

In the Aberdeen study, the practice with the enthusiastic
doctors achieved the highest response rate; 79 per cent atten-

ded. However, this practice also contained proportionately more women from the higher social classes. The detection rate was 0·4 per cent. In the practice where enthusiasm was less marked a lower response rate was achieved, but the detection rate among those examined was more than twice as high (0·9 per cent). Both differences may have been associated with a different social class distribution. The third practice was considered to be of a social class distribution comparable with the second and showed a similar detection rate (0·9 per cent). The proportion of responders to postal invitations was similar to that in the second practice. Women who did not attend were subsequently interviewed and invited to give their reasons. Very few expressed any specific reason beyond a general lack of interest but a few stated their dislike of doctors or of hospitals and a few said that they did not wish to know if they had cancer. It is, of course, a serious problem that such tests never permit an assurance to be given that cancer is not present, nor that it will not develop. A similar problem has been reported in relation to chest radiography surveys among unsophisticated Maori populations; tests which produce positive findings may be seen as causing them, while negative findings cannot be interpreted as guaranteeing health.

The early findings in Aberdeen have prompted a more general scrutiny of the determinants of non-response to offers of cervical cytological examination.

Wakefield and Sansom[88] reported a description of women who respond to the invitation to undergo cytological examination. More than half of the 4,963 women in their sample had been examined in either local authority or family planning clinics. Two-thirds of the women were under forty years old; less than one tenth were over fifty years of age. Even among women referred from general practitioners, fewer than one fifth were over 45 years old. Comparison of the social class distribution of responders with that in the related population confirmed the findings of earlier studies that the lower social classes are grossly under-represented among responders. It is clear that the older women of the lower social classes do not respond well to current techniques used to persuade them to undergo cytological examination. Yet it is precisely these categories of women who have the highest rate of positive test results and the highest rate of mortality from cancer of the uterine cervix. Thus, neither specifically directed invitations nor offers made in the context of the necessity for vaginal examination for other causes are likely to secure the widespread examination of the women who are most at risk of cancer of the cervix, unless some means is determined for ensuring a better coverage of the susceptible groups.

Studies of the barriers to response are currently in progress (e.g. by Wakefield and his colleagues in Britain) and some preliminary data have been reported. It already seems clear that a simple factual knowledge of the issues involved is not sufficient to ensure response even where this knowledge exists. Behaviour in this respect is motivated not only by relatively simple fears of having 'cancer' detected and by a sense of modesty with respect to vaginal examination, but also by less articulate but more deep-seated fears of the possible damage to sexual and reproductive function that the procedure might entail as well as by simple inertia in responding to an unfamiliar situation. It also seems likely that lack of effective communication between patients and their doctor is an important barrier to the effective operation of this as of so many other procedures in personal preventive medicine.

Cancer is perhaps a special problem since public fears of this disease are not only almost universal but are to a great extent based on a still unfavourable outlook. But many far more tractable diseases are permitted to cause unnecessary permanent disability and death because they are not brought to medical attention at a stage when intervention might have been effective. In many cases, such as in progressive locomotor and other disease in the elderly, the causes are more complex than they may seem at first sight. For example, social isolation is a widely reported concomitant of ageing and although it may to some extent be a simple function of the residential mobility of the younger generation which leaves the elderly person little choice, there is increasing evidence that it contains a large element of social disengagement which arises from psychological processes associated with ageing. Such isolation, along with the tendency to accept impairment of health as a concomitant of ageing, and the mental deterioration which so frequently accompanies ageing among the socially isolated, can lead to failure to report symptoms which might have led to the institution of effective treatment. Our health services offer very little in the way of preventive surveillance of the increasingly large elderly population and a survey of disability carried out among the elderly patients of three Scottish general practices[16] showed how difficult it is to maintain an effective surveillance in an urban population.

But it is extremely difficult to maintain an adequate surveillance of early and minor ill-health even among a population of working adults. Doctors and patients do not agree about what constitutes an appropriate occasion for the one to approach the other, and this lack of agreement leads to a marked lack of patience with the expectations of each from the other. The lack of communication is further complicated by differences of class and education. Thus the views of patients and their doctors concerning the nature of health and their respective responsibilities for maintaining it are often confused to the point of grossly hindering the effective application of available medical skill and knowledge.

Studies of these problems have only recently been begun in Western European and North American society although they have been intensively examined in relation to the impact of Western medicine on developing societies. Although they may be thought of as a special example of the study of the cultural impact of technological change, it is also clear that studies of the specifically medical issues will be required if we are to make a fully effective use of the resources of modern medicine.

Chapter 12   Social medicine and medical science

AT the beginning of this book we traced the development of social medicine as a science and considered how the changing needs of human society, the growth of ideas about the determinants of community health and the development of methods of enquiry combined to establish social medicine as an academic discipline concerned with the distribution of health and sickness in human society and with the origins and the consequences of the patterns that are discernible. In the chapters that followed we considered the principal sources of relevant data and the methods of enquiry in use at the present time and considered a series of examples of recent and current research into the areas that seem particularly relevant to present needs and interests. It now remains to consider the relevance of this science to medicine in general, its place in medical education and its possible future contribution to medical science and practice.

It may be useful to begin by considering the relationship of social medicine to preventive medicine since the terms are frequently conjoined in the titles of academic departments and in sections of the undergraduate medical curriculum both in Britain and elsewhere. Preventive medicine, as its name implies, is a branch of medical practice concerned with the development and employment of measures capable of averting the onset of disease. In the nineteenth century, when its period of most spectacular development occurred, the diseases that most intruded on public awareness were the acute communicable diseases that depended on the transmission of microorganisms from person to person. Such transmission sometimes occurred directly and was best prevented by isolation of infected persons. In other cases it occurred more deviously by the contamination of food or water or via some vector animal such as the fly or the mosquito, capable of carrying infection between person and person; interruption of transmission in these more complicated cases called for organized community effort. Preventive medicine had therefore largely to be carried out by public agencies having the authority to curtail liberty and to organize the disposal of wastes or the control of vector species. At this time, these considerations seemed to distinguish preventive medicine rather sharply from curative medicine which, being relatively ineffective, could safely be left to private arrangement. Thus preventive medicine became closely associated in the public and professional mind with public or community health. As an academic discipline, social medicine is the heir to public health and in medical schools has often inherited also the associated title implying an especial concern with preventive medicine.

There are several reasons why the particular association is no longer useful. The first is that preventive medicine is no longer uniquely distinguishable as being a public concern. All medicine is now generally accepted as being involved with the public health, and the provision of all kinds of health and medical care is accepted in most communities as a general social concern. It is also now generally the case that such diseases as may be preventable are as likely to be preventable by intervention directed at selected individuals as by communally directed measures. This first arose with the introduction of specific immunization procedures but it now applies to many preventive measures. For example, the prevention of lung cancer may depend in future on specifically directed advice to individuals identifiable as being at especial risk. Another consideration is that many of the diseases that are socially important may be difficult to prevent and yet easy to treat. The proverbial superiority of prevention over cure dates from a time when curative medicine was far less effective than preventive and when the diseases that men feared were clearly recognizable as being in principal avoidable. Many important diseases of today are not actually avoidable, being inescapable manifestations of the processes of ageing or adaptation. For many diseases of slow, inevitable and insidious onset, the distinction between prevention and intervention is impossible to make. In fact, medicine has become interventive rather than specifically preventive or curative since it is concerned to intervene at the most effective point in the chain of causally related processes which comprise the development, onset and resolution of disease.

In the now substantial areas of the chronic, degenerative, neoplastic and mental diseases, an interventive approach is likely to continue to be the principal combative means at our disposal. It becomes particularly important, therefore, that we should understand as clearly as possible how best we may mobilize our interventive resources and at what point in the chain of events it is possible or most profitable to intervene. Social medicine inherits from the older discipline of public health this concern with problems of mobilization of resources and with the provision of an understanding of the principles on which effective mobilization may be based.

Medicine is a communal resource, applicable to the health problems which confront society. The task of defining these problems, of enhancing our understanding of them and of effectively deploying our resources in their solution is the central pre-occupation in social medicine. As we have seen, the range of investigations appropriate to such a central pre-occupation is extensive and the range of techniques that require to be deployed is not only wide but often extends beyond that traditionally associated with medical enquiry and dealt with in medical curricula. Social medicine therefore calls on a range of skills and personnel which reach beyond the medical profession itself, and research relevant to the field is often carried out in academic departments having little, if any, connexion with a medical school. Since social medicine may embrace studies of the sociology of medicine, the economics of medicine, or the administration of medicine, it is not surprising that studies relevant to social medicine may often be carried out in academic departments of sociology, economics or administration.

Parallel situations are encountered, of course, throughout the academic world. The theory and practice of medicine has for long been heavily dependent on discoveries made by chemists, physicists or general biologists. But it is new for medicine to find itself involved with the behavioural sciences in whose basic principles few medical men have received any instruction whatsoever.

The most important responsibility of an academic department in a university is the systematization of knowledge within its field. Few departments in modern universities could claim a comprehensive research cover of the area of knowledge subsumed under their formal titles and few would wish to become involved in demarcation disputes over areas of research. The continuing utility of distinct academic departments and disciplines rests on the need for collation and appraisal of new knowledge and for its systematic communication to a new generation of students. This academic function is especially relevant in the case of the department of social medicine since the new knowledge that is important arises from so wide a field and one which is often unfamiliar to medical men and medical students.

In the examples used to illustrate the characteristic scope of research in social medicine, we considered research into the causation of disease and research into the functioning of the services with which we deal with diseases. Present problems were considered as lying in the areas of the constitutional causation of disease, the controllable environment and the effect of human behaviour on the genesis and nature of disease and the effectiveness with which it may be diagnosed and treated. It may now be useful to consider these themes for the light they throw on the future importance of our subject and its likely development.

One of the most important problems of aetiological research at the present time and in the likely future is the change that has occurred in the distinction between health and disease. The acute diseases with which medicine used to be principally concerned represented clearly distinguishable departures from health which usually culminated either in death or in a return to health. Many diseases of today represent simply the extreme values of a continuously distributable variable whose central values are compatible with health. For example, arterial pressure, nutritional state, intelligence, or pulmonary function are attributes in respect of which humans vary and in respect of which extreme values constitute disease. This poses important problems. The distinction between health and disease is essentially arbitrary and rests mainly on a consensus of what is acceptable. Levels of unacceptability may vary between populations as well as among different individuals within a population.

The particular concern of social medicine with diseases of this kind is obvious. In the first place, their understanding calls for studies of the population distribution of the relevant attributes and their associated variables; in the second place, the problem of disease definition and its dependence on factors associated with definable groups within populations relates such studies, both conceptually and methodologically, to those in other social sciences.

The study of health in populations thus requires consideration of a diverse range of factors which determine the distributions of the related biological variables as well as prevalent levels of acceptability of the relative handicap with which they are associated. For example, pulmonary function varies continuously between the extremes represented on the one hand by the Olympic athlete and on the other by the patient immobilized by bronchitis. Most of us are living under a considerable disability when compared with a marathon runner and for most of us the disability is irremediable. It is the modest level of our aspirations that leads to our regarding ourselves as healthy. Similarly, whole nations and classes of mankind accept levels of health far below those which would be tolerable to young, middle class adults in Western Europe. Even in Western Europe we accept quite philosophically a level of prenatal mortality which we should be quite unwilling to tolerate if it occurred in post-natal life. Health is not a clearly definable condition independent of its social, economic and historical context.

These considerations imply the need to study health as a population variable and to integrate the findings of many different social and biological enquiries if we are to understand the determinants of the prevalent levels of health in societies. It is still true to say that much research in social medicine is handicapped by concepts of health and sickness as distinct, antithetical states between which an individual may pass for simple, clearly definable reasons.

Concepts of this kind underlie the unfortunate preoccupation of some epidemiologists with the problem of analysing data on the population occurrence of disease with a view to identifying what may be thought of as causal agents in the hope that they will turn out to be simple physical substances or micro-organisms. For example, far more time and money has been expended on the search for chemical substances in cigarette smoke which will produce cancer in laboratory animals than in trying to explain why people prefer to smoke even although they may risk an unpleasant death by doing so. Conceptually, the former kind of research is easier; technically, both kinds of work may be difficult, time-consuming and expensive. But the latter is far more obviously relevant to the problem of lung cancer in human populations.

Social medicine has an important contribution to make to medical education in that it continually demonstrates the relevance of research outside the laboratory. The early concentration in the undergraduate curriculum on the laboratory sciences and the use in medical practice of laboratory findings as a final arbiter of diagnostic problems imbues the medical scientist with an excessive tendency to cling to the laboratory bench and to avoid problems which do not lend themselves to solution by means of test-tube, microscope and experimental animal. But aside from social medicine enquiry, there are many problems which might be better tackled by the rigorous and systematic study of patients and their progress. The evaluation of treatment in terms of its contribution to the patient's future life and the relative importance of the various signs and symptoms in the diagnostic and prognostic processes as well as in the taxonomy of disease are areas generally neglected by medical science.

But perhaps the most important contribution that the development of social medicine may make to medicine in general is its re-integration with the biological sciences that study the ecology of species, the sources of their variation,

and the determinants of their survival. Sociology and demo-
graphy have much more in common with general biology
than has much of modern medical science whose affinities
are often more with physics, chemistry and engineering. One
would not wish to despise such affinities, but only to regret
that they have often led to the loss of older, valuable medical
traditions.

References

1. GREENWOOD, G. (1932) *Epidemiology: Historical and Experimental*, Johns Hopkins Press, Baltimore.
2. McKEOWN, T. (1961) *Millbank Memorial Fund Quarterly*, Vol. XXXIX, p. 594.
3. ACHESON, E. D. (1964) *Brit. J. preventive and social medicine*, Vol. 18, p. 8.
4. SMITH, A. AND MACDONALD, I. S. (1965) *Health Bulletin*, Vol. XXIII, p. 42.
5. e.g. LECK, I. AND MILLAR, E. L. M. (1963) *Brit. J. prev. soc. Med.*, Vol. 17, p. 1.
6. e.g. COCHRANE, A. (1965) *Millbank Memorial Fund Quarterly*, Vol. XLIII, p. 326.
7. FLETCHER, C. M. AND OLDHAM, P. D. (1959) in *Medical Surveys and Clinical Trials*, London.
8. HIGGINS, I. T. T. (1958) in *Recent Studies in Epidemiology*, Blackwell.
9. JEFFERYS, M. (1959) *Communication to Society for Social Medicine*.
10. MACGREGOR, E. AND BAIRD, D. (1963) *British Medical J.*, Vol. 1., p. 1631.
11. COLEMAN, J., MENZEL, H. AND KATZ, E. (1959) *Journal of Chronic Diseases*, Vol. 9, p. 1.
12. ELLIS, A. W. M. (1942) *Lancet*, Vol. I, pp. 1, 34 and 72.
13. McKEOWN, T. AND BROWN, R. G. (1955) *Population Studies*, Vol. 9, p. 119.
14. McKEOWN, T. (1961) *New England Journal of Medicine*, Vol. 264, p. 594.
15. SMITH, A. (1961) *Supplement to Annual Report of the Registrar General for Scotland for 1961*.
16. WILLIAMSON, J., STOKOE, J. H. AND OTHERS, (1964) *Lancet*, Vol. 1, p. 1117.
17. PEARSON, K. AND JAEDERHOLM, G. A. (1914) *On the Continuity of Mental Defect*, Duncan & Co. London.
18. LEWIS, E. O. (1933) *Journal of Mental Science*, Vol. 79, p. 298.
19. ROBERTS, J. A. F. (1950) *Congres Internationale de psychiatrie*, Vol. VI, p. 55.
20. VERNON, P. E. (1955) *Bulletin of the British Psychological Society*, Vol. 26, p. 1.
21. WEITZ, W. (1923) *Zeitschrift Klinische Med.*, Vol. 96, p. 151.
22. PICKERING, G. (1963) in *Epidemiology: Reports on Research and Teaching*, O.U.P.
23. PLATT, R. (1959) *Lancet*, Vol. II, p. 55.

24. BROWN, R. G., McKEOWN, T. AND WHITFIELD, A. G. W. (1957) *Can. J. Biochem. Physiol.,* Vol. 35, p. 897.
25. YLPPö (1920) *Zeitschrift fur Kinderheilkunde,* Vol. 24, p. 1.
26. GIBSON, J. R. AND McKEOWN, T. (1950) *Brit. J. social Med.,* Vol. 4, p. 221.
27. McKEOWN, T. AND GIBSON, J. R. (1951), *Brit. J. soc. Med.,* Vol. 5, p. 98.
28. McKEOWN, T. AND RECORD, R. G. (1952) *Journal of Endocrinology,* Vol. 8, p. 386.
29. McKEOWN, T. AND RECORD R. G. (1953) *J. Endoc.,* Vol. 9, p. 418.
30. McKEOWN, T. AND RECORD, R. G. (1953) *J. Endoc.,* Vol. 10, p. 73.
31. CAWLEY, R. H., McKEOWN, T. AND RECORD, R. G. (1954), *American Journal of Human Genetics,* Vol. 6, p. 448.
32. RECORD, R. G. (1961) *Brit. J. prev. soc. Med.,* Vol. 15, p. 93.
33. EDWARDS, J. H. (1958) *Brit. J. prev. soc. Med.,* Vol. 12, p. 115.
34. e.g. INGALLS, T. H., PUGH, T. F. AND MacMAHON, B. (1954). *Brit. J. prev. soc. Med.,* Vol. 8, p. 17.
35. e.g. COFFEY, V. P. AND JESSOP, W. J. E. (1959) *Lancet,* Vol. II, p. 395.
36. McKEOWN T. AND RECORD, R. G. (1951) *Lancet,* Vol. 1, p. 192.
37. LECK, I. (1961) *Unpublished contribution to Society for Social Medicine.*
38. SMITH, A. (1963) *British J. prev. soc. Med.,* Vol. 17, p. 185.
39. COURT BROWN, W. M. AND DOLL, W. R. S. (1957), *M.R.C. Special Report Series No. 295,* H.M.S.O.
40. STEWART, A., WEBB, J. AND OTHERS (1958) *Lancet,* Vol. II, p. 447.
41. STEWART, A., WEBB, J. AND HEWITT, D. (1958) *Brit. med. J.,* Vol. 1, p. 1495.
42. COURT BROWN, W. M., DOLL, W. R. S. AND HILL, A. B. (1960) *Brit. med. J.,* Vol. II, p. 1539.
43. MacMAHON, B. (1962) *Journal of the National Cancer Inst.,* Vol. 28, p. 1173.
44. DOLL, W. R. S. AND HILL, A. B. (1952) *British Medical Journal,* Vol. II, p. 739.
45. DOLL, W. R. S. AND HILL, A. B. (1956) *British Medical Journal,* Vol. II, p. 1071.
46. HAMMOND, E. C. AND HORN, D. (1958) *Journal of the American Medical Association,* Vol. 166, pp. 1159 and 1294.
47. WYNDER, E. L., LEMON, F. R. AND BROSS, I. J. (1959) *Cancer,* Vol. 12, p. 1016.
48. KREYBERG, L. (1956) *British Journal of preventive and social Medicine,* Vol. 10, p. 145.
49. EDWARDS, J. H. (1957) *British Journal of preventive and social Medicine,* Vol. 11, p. 10.
50. CARTWRIGHT, A., MARTIN, F. M. AND THOMPSON, J. G. (1960) *Lancet,* Vol. I, p. 327.

51. JEFFERYS, M. AND WESTAWAY, W. R. (1961) *Health Education Journal*, Vol. 19, p. 3.
52. SMITH, A. (1963) *Supplement to the Annual Report of the Registrar General for Scotland*, 1963.
53. KISSEN, D. (1963 and 1964) *British J. of Medical Psychology*, Vol. 36, p. 27, and Vol. 37, p. 203.
54. STOCKS, P. (1951) *Lancet*, Vol. I, p. 351.
55. MORRIS, J. N., HEADY, J. A. AND OTHERS (1953) *Lancet*, Vol. II, p. 1053.
56. MORRIS, J. N. AND CRAWFORD, J. G. (1958) *British Medical Journal*, Vol. II, p. 1485.
57. ARNEIL, G. C. (1964) *Practitioner*, Vol. 192, p. 652.
58. HAMILTON F. M. W. AND TAYLOR, E. C. (1966) *Unpublished communication to Society for Social Medicine*.
59. KEYS, A. AND GRANDE, F. (1957) *Amer. J. pub. Hlth.*, Vol. 47, p. 1520.
60. DAWBER, T. R., KANNEL, W. B. AND OTHERS (1962) *Proceedings of the Royal Society of Medicine*, Vol. 55, p. 265.
61. ENOS, W. F., HOLMES, R. H. AND BAYER, J. C. (1953) *J. of the American Medical Association*, Vol. 152, p. 1090.
62. MCKINLAY, P. L. (1960) *Health Bulletin* Vol. XVIII, p. 25.
63. CROFTON, E. AND CROFTON, J. (1963) *Brit. med. J.*, Vol. 2, p. 1161.
64. HEWITT, D. (1956) *British J. prev. soc. Med.*, Vol. 10, p. 45.
65. DOUGLAS, J. W. B. AND WALLER, R. E. (1966) *Brit. J. prev. soc. Med.*, Vol. 20, p. 1.
66. HARNETT, R. W. F. AND MAIR, A. (1963) *Scottish Medical Journal*, Vol. 8, p. 175.
67. MEADOWS, S. H. (1961) *Brit. J. prev. soc. Med.*, Vol. 15, p. 171.
68. FAIRBAIRN, A. S. AND REID, D. D. (1958) *Brit. J. prev. soc. Med.*, Vol. 12, p. 94.
69. OSWALD, N. C. AND MEDVEI, V. C. (1955) *Lancet*, Vol. II, p. 843.
70. PUGH, T. F. AND MACMAHON, B. (1962) *Epidemiologic Findings in U.S. Mental Hospital Data*, Little Brown, Boston.
71. SMITH, A. AND CARSTAIRS, V. (1966) *Patients under Psychiatric Care in Hospital: Scotland 1963*, H.M.S.O.
72. CAMERON, D. (1954) *British J. prev. soc. Med.*, Vol. 8, p. 180.
73. LOWE, C. R. AND GARRATT, F. N. (1959) *Brit. J. prev. soc. Med.*, Vol. 13, p. 88.
74. HOLLINGSHEAD, A. B. AND REDLICH, F. C. (1953) *American Sociological Review*, Vol. 18, p. 163.
75. MORRISON, S. L. (1959) *J. Mental Science*, Vol. 105, p. 999.
76. HARE, E. H. (1956) *J. Mental Science*, Vol. 102, p. 349.
77. COOPER, B. (1961) *Brit. J. prev. soc. Med.*, Vol. 15, pp. 17 and 31.
78. BROWN, G. W., MONCK, E. M. AND OTHERS (1962) *British J. prev. soc. Med.*, Vol. 16, p. 55.
79. MARTIN, F. M., BROTHERSTON, J. H. F. AND CHARE, S. P. W. (1951) *Brit. J. prev. soc. Med.*, Vol. 11, p. 196.

80. LOGAN, W. P. D. (1953 and 1955) *Studies in Medical and Population Subjects, Nos. 7 and 9*, H.M.S.O.
81. BECKER, H. S., HUGHES, E. C. AND OTHERS (1961) *Boys in White, Student Culture in Medical School*, Univ. of Chicago Press.
82. FOX, R. C. (1957) in *The Student Physician* edited by Merton, R. K., Reader, G. and Kendall, P. L., Harvard University Press.
83. MARTIN, F. M. (1966) *Paper given to World Congress of Sociology at Evian*, France.
84. PETERSON, O. L., ANDREWS, L. P. AND OTHERS (1956) *Journal medical Education*, Vol. 31, pt. 2.
85. MARTIN, F. M. AND BODDY, F. A. (1962) in *The Sociological Review Monograph No. 5*.
86. JEFFERYS, M. AND ELLIOTT, P. M. (1966) *Women in Medicine*, Office of Health Economics.
87. RICHARDS, I. D. G. AND LOWE, C. R. (1966), *Lancet*, Vol. I, p. 1169.
88. WAKEFIELD, J. AND SANSOM, C. D. (1966) *The Medical Officer*, Vol. CXVI, p. 145.

Index

Abortion, 112
Ageing and Disease, 87, 206
Age specific mortality, 45–46
Anencephaly, 120–125
Association for the Study of Medical Education, 190–192
Automation of record keeping, 76

Behaviour and Disease, 93, 133–148
Bills of Mortality, 16
Biology and Social Medicine, 213–214
Blood groups, 98–99
Broad St. pump, 17
Bronchitis and air pollution, 163–165
Bronchitis and cigarette smoking, 161, 165
Bronchitis in London Boroughs, 161–164
Bronchitis in postal workers, 164–165
Brownlee, 18
Budd, William, 17

Cancer Registration, 34
Cause of Diseases, 27–29
Causes of Death—changes, 84
Censuses, 79–80
Census of psychiatric in-patients, 167–169
Cervical cytology, 203–206
Cholesterol, 156–158
Cigarette smoking, 22
Cigarette smoking and bronchitis, 161, 165
Cigarette smoking and lung cancer, 133–141
Clinical Medicine—distinguished from Social Medicine, 12
Coal for domestic heating, 149
Cohort mortality, 53–54

Cohort mortality from bonchitis, 160–161
Cohort mortality in lung cancer, 134, 140
Communication between Doctor and patient, 207
Community mental health, 182–185
Computers in Social Medicine, 38–39, 75
Congenital malformations, 34–35
Continuous data collection, 24–39
Coronary artery disease and activity, 142–148
Coronary artery disease in transport workers, 144–145

Death Certificate, 31–32
Delivery in hospital, 198–202
Development of Social Medicine, 11–23
Disease classification, 54–58
Dysgenic effects of medicine, 109

Ecological epidemiology, 19
Ecology, 213
Epidemic—connexion with epidemiology, 12
Epidemiology—definition, 11
Evaluation of services, 29–30
Exercise and heart disease, 142–148
Expectation of life, 51–53

Familial concentration of disease, 97–98
Familial incidence of stillbirths, 124
Farr, William, 17–18
Fatty acids, 157–158
Foetal growth in multiple pregnancy, 116
Food, 150–159
Food consumption, 152–153
Food supply, 150–151

Framingham, Massachusetts, 67–68, 156–157
Frost, W. H., 18

Galen, 15
General Register Office, 16
Genetics and preventive medicine, 110–111
Gestation and birth weight, 115–120
Graded characteristics, 70–71
Graunt, 15–16
Greenwood, 14

Hardy-Weinberg Law, 108
Hippocrates, 14
Hiroshima, 125
Hospital statistics, 34
Host, agent and environment, 19
Hypertension, 70, 104–106

Immigrants and mental illness, 107
Incidence rates, 41–44
Industry—toxic and accident risks, 20, 27–28
Infant mortality rates, 48–49
Influenza—1919 Epidemic, 19
Influenza and anencephaly, 122
Inheritance and intelligence, 102–104
International Statistical Classification of Diseases, 56–58

Koch, R., 19
Korean War—Autopsy findings, 157

Leukaemia—and ankylosing spondylitis, 126
Leukaemia and X-rays, 63, 126–132
Liberal traditions in medicine, 11
Life tables, 51–53
Lung cancer and smoking, 133–141

Malformations of the C.N.S., 120–125
Man—as an animal for genetic research, 94

Mating patterns, 109
Medical care research, 186–207
Medical education, 188–195
Medical manpower, 193–195
Medical students, 188–192
Mental hospital admission rates, 170–174
Mental hospital populations, 167–170
Mental illness, 90, 166–185
Mental illness and marital state, 169
Methods of analysis, 40–60
Morbidity in old age, 207
Morbidity statistics, 33–39
Mortality rates, 44–54
Mortality statistics, 30–33
Multifactorial inheritance, 100–107
Mutations, 96–97

National Food Survey, 152–153
Neonatal mortality rate, 49
Neurosis in a new housing estate, 182–185
Notification of disease, 33
Nutrition and disease, 150–159

Occupational classification, 58–59
Organization of medical care, 195–203

Patterns of disease—present and past, 83–92
Pearson, Karl, 18
Perinatal mortality, 89
Perinatal mortality rates, 51
Personal Doctor, 92–93
Physical environment and disease, 149–165
Pigmentation of skin, 97, 109
Planning of services, 24–27
Pollution of atmosphere, 159–165
Population growth, 79–82
Post-neonatal mortality rate, 49
Pregnancy wastage, 112–120
Prematurity, 114–120
Prenatal environment, 112–132
Present and future health problems, 79–93

Prevalence rates, 42–44
Prevalence studies, 68
Prevention of heart disease, 148, 159
Preventive medicine, 91, 208–210
Primitive social medicine, 13
Prognosis in schizophrenia, 176–179

Rates, 41–54
Record linkage, 38, 124–125
Representativeness of samples, 62–64
Respiratory symptom questionnaire, 159
Retrolental fibroplasia, 29
Retrospective versus prospective enquiries, 63, 125–132
Rickets, 153–155
Rise in mental hospital admission rates, 170–171
Ross, Ronald, 17

Sampling, 62–68
Schizophrenia, 169, 173, 174–182
Schizophrenia and family background, 179–182
Seasonal variation in disease incidence, 122–123
Sex differences in coronary artery disease, 144
Sex differences in foetal growth, 115, 119
Sickle cells, 99–100
Sin and disease, 13
Smallpox, 28

Snow, John, 17
Social class, 59
Social class and anencephaly, 123
Social class and coronary artery disease, 144–145
Social class and prognosis, 176–178
Social class and schizophrenia, 174–179
Social class drift and bronchitis, 164
Social class drift and schizophrenia, 175
Social variables etc., 72–74
Special surveys, 61–76
Speed limits, 149
Standardized mortality ratio, 46–48
Stillbirth rates, 50
Stillbirth rates—recent trends, 202
Stillbirths from anencephaly, 120–125
Surveys—continuous health, 35–36
Surveys—national interview, 36–38
Sydenham, 15
Symptom questionnaires, 68–69

Tuberculosis, 19
Types of national and regional health data, 30–29

Uptake of medical care, 203–207
Uses of continuous data, 24–30

Vitamin D, 153–155

Women medical graduates, 193–195

X-rays and leukaemia, 126–132